WITHDRAWN

Emotion, Character, and Responsibility

Emotion, Character, and Responsibility

John Sabini

Maury Silver

New York   Oxford
Oxford University Press
1998

Oxford University Press

Oxford New York
Athens Auckland Bangkok Bogotá Buenos Aires Calcutta
Cape Town Chennai Dar es Salaam Delhi Florence Hong Kong Istanbul
Karachi Kuala Lumpur Madrid Melbourne Mexico City Mumbai
Nairobi Paris São Paulo Singapore Taipei Tokyo Toronto Warsaw

and associated companies in
Berlin Ibadan

Copyright © 1998 by Oxford University Press, Inc.

Published by Oxford University Press, Inc.
198 Madison Avenue, New York, New York 10016

Oxford is a registered trademark of Oxford University Press

All rights reserved. No part of this publication may be reproduced,
stored in a retrieval system, or transmitted, in any form or by any means,
electronic, mechanical, photocopying, recording, or otherwise,
without the prior permission of Oxford University Press.

Library of Congress Cataloging-in-Publication Data
Sabini, John, 1947–
Emotion, character, and responsibility / John Sabini, Maury Silver.
p. cm
Includes bibliographical references and index.
ISBN 0-19-512167-8
1. Emotions. 2. Character. 3. Responsibility. I. Silver,
Maury, 1944– . II. Title.
BF531.S23 1998
152.4—dc21   98-19103

1 3 5 7 9 8 6 4 2
Printed in the United States of America
on acid-free paper

Acknowledgments

Chapter 2 draws on material previously published as Sabini, J., & Silver, M. (1987) Emotions, responsibility and character. In F. Schoeman (Ed.), *Character, responsibility and the emotions*. New York: Cambridge University Press; and Sabini, J., & Silver, M. (1987). Character: The moral and the aesthetic. *International Journal of Moral and Social Studies, 2*, 189–201.

Chapter 3 appeared as Sabini, J., & Silver, M. (1985). On the captivity of the will: Sympathy, caring, and a moral sense of the human. *Journal for the Theory of Social Behaviour, 15*, 23–37.

Chapter 4 appeared as Silver, M., and Sabini, J. (1985). Sincerity: Feelings and constructions in making a self. In K. Gergen and K. Davis (Eds.), *The social construction of the person*. New York: Springer-Verlag.

Chapter 5 appeared as Sabini, J., & Silver, M. (1989). Loyalty as good and duty: A critique of Stocker. *International Journal of Moral and Social Studies, 4,* 131–138.

Chapter 6 appeared as Sabini, J., & Silver, M. (1997). In defense of shame: shame in the context of guilt and embarrassment. *Journal for the Theory of Social Behaviour. 27,* 1–15.

Chapter 7 appeared as Silver, M., Sabini, J., & Miceli, M. (1989). On knowing self-deception. *Journal for the Theory of Social Behaviour, 19,* 213–227.

Chapter 8 appeared as Sabini, J., & Silver, M. (1996). On the possible non-existence of emotions: The passions. *Journal for the Theory of Social Behaviour. 26,* 375–398.

Contents

1. Introduction   3

2. Emotion, Responsibility, and Character   9

3. On the Captivity of the Will: Sympathy, Caring, and a Moral Sense of the Human   31

4. Sincerity: Feelings and Constructions in Making a Self   53

5. Loyalty as Good and Duty: A Critique of Stocker   69

6. In Defense of Shame: Shame in the Context of Guilt and Embarrassment   81

7. On Knowing Self-Deception   105

8. On the Possible Nonexistence of Emotions: The Passions   129

   Index   167

Emotion, Character, and Responsibility

1

Introduction

A computer is behind one door; a human is behind another. You must decide which door hides the human. You can ask any questions you like for as long as you like. The answers are printed. This is the Turing test. According to Alan Turing, if you can't distinguish the two, then you have no grounds for treating the computer as other than a person. At the moment there is no machine that could seriously take the test, but it's interesting to consider what Turing and others *believe* would be the machine's undoing—what do they think is so intrinsically human that a machine couldn't have it and still be a machine? Turing didn't believe that anything need separate the machine from the person, but he considered important candidates for machine disability, and quotes G. Jefferson, "Not until a machine can write a sonnet or compose a concerto because of thoughts and emotions felt. . . . No mechanism could feel (and not merely artificially signal, an easy contrivance) pleasure at its successes, grief when its valves fuse, be warmed by flattery, be made miserable by its mistakes, be charmed by sex, be angry or depressed when it cannot get what it wants" (Turing, 1950, in Hofstadter & Dennett, 1981, p. 60). Turing, contrary to Jefferson, was optimistic about a machine's some day having the emotional intelligence necessary to write a sonnet, but he agreed with Jefferson that if a machine couldn't display emotions then it would flunk the Turing test in a nontrivial way (also cf. Hofstadter, 1996, and Hofstadter & Dennet, 1981, who makes the argument with regard to a chess-playing computer). For both Turing and Jefferson, then, emotional experience is criterial to being a person.

Turing's and Jefferson's making emotional central—or at least necessary—to the question of whether something is or is not a person seems both obvious and odd. It seems obvious in the sense that the intuition that part of what it is to be human is to have emotions is very widely shared among computer scientists as well as romantic poets. But it is also odd—odd because traditional accounts of what it is to be human, at least those that don't stop at featherless bipeds, stress choice and rationality as the essence of personhood. Surely any account of human nature intended to articulate our moral sensibilities must stress choice and rationality. And emotions do not fit in any obvious way with choice and rationality; indeed, they seem to be the antithesis of these hallmarks of the human. Our aim in the essays collected here is to reconcile these two intuitions; we aim to show specifically why emotions are important in our conception of a person's character.

One way to reconcile our intuition that emotions are important with our intuition that what is important about a person is what she decides to do with what she chooses is by claiming, as Sartre has (1948), that having an emotion is a matter of making a choice. On this view, there is no conflict between the idea that what is important about a person is what she chooses and what is important about a person is the emotions she feels, since the emotions felt wind up being examples of choices made. But we will not take this path.

The reason we reject Sartre's reconciliation is that ordinarily when people describe an experience as emotional they imply that it is to an extent beyond the will, passive, a reaction as opposed to an action. (This is, of course, why Kant and other moral theorists were so uneasy with the idea that emotions are relevant to character.) We accept this idea; we accept the idea that to have, to *really* have, an emotion is to be its passive 'victim'. One of our purposes in writing this book is to examine the role the concept of passivity plays in our understanding of character. As we shall see (in chapter 2, on "Emotion, Character, and Responsibility"), coming to grips with the passive nature of important aspects of our experience will force the realization that character is more than moral, that there are aesthetic as well as moral aspects of character. In chapter 3, "On the Captivity of the Will," we argue for another significant place for passivity in human nature: our sympathy for the suffering of others, sympathy for their pain, or for their having their emotion or emotions violated, is connected with our sense that their suffering is beyond their control, or passive.

One aspect of rationality, especially as it applies to morality, is impartiality: morality shouldn't play favorites—any worthy person deserves to be helped. Our emotions are not impartial. Presumably we do not love all people equally. And, more important, we don't even love equally deserving-to-be-loved people equally. Worst of all—at least from some points of view—we might all have been willing to admit that Mother Theresa was a more deserving person than our own mothers are, but who among us would have pitched our own mother out of the lifeboat to make room for Mother Teresa? Who among us would be that disloyal? In chapter 5, on loyalty, we show how acting from loyalty can be reconciled with the traditional accounts of acting out of duty, even though loyalty seems an awful candidate for a morally relevant concept.

In the chapters we have discussed so far we have not been concerned to analyze the notion of emotion per se. We haven't said what an emotion is. Surely an important idea that we all have about emotions is that they are feelings. But this idea causes great trouble, for several reasons. The most important is that it is hard to see how emotions could be both feelings and important. After all, itches are feelings and they're not very important. In subsequent chapters we are focally concerned with the issue of what role emotions, as feelings and otherwise, play in our judgments of the people who have them.

Our most direct approach to the role of feelings in the understanding of character is in chapter 4, on sincerity, where we confront a fact that we, up to this point, have managed to avoid: emotion terms have dual uses, dispositional and episodic. I may truly "feel love for Judy" in her presence—the episodic sense of love—but if I abandon her to the depredations of terrorists because I have a movie I want to see, surely you wouldn't say that I really loved Judy (dispositional sense). The senses are connected, of course. In that chapter (chapter 4) we examine the sincerity of emotion reports in terms of the interplay between these two senses of the emotions.

Shame and guilt are the emotions that are most directly involved in a moral or aesthetic appraisal of the self. For this reason they have their own chapter (chapter 6). Shame, guilt, and embarrassment all flow from the recognition that one has strayed. It is perennially attractive to tie morality tightly to these emotions. But at least one reason not to do that is the fact that people are sometimes quite skilled at avoiding a recognition that they are doing something shameful. So one reason not to want morality and emotion directly connected is the phenomenon of self-deception, a cause of much philosophical and psychological confusion and skepticism. Chapter 7, on self-deception, shows how it is possible to fool our selves into not recognizing and not experiencing a tarnished self.

In the chapters we have discussed so far, we consider the relations of the emotions to character, aesthetics, morality, and so on. In chapter 8, on the nature of the emotions, we focus more narrowly on the role of the emotions in our psychology; we ask especially what the relation of emotion to motivation is. We believe that this perspective allows us to see how emotions can play the role we have argued they play in previous chapters.

References

Turing, A. (1950). Computing machinery and intelligence. Reprinted in: Hofstadter, D. R., & Dennett, D. C. (Eds.) (1982). *The mind's I: fantasies and reflections on self and soul.* New York: Bantam Book. (Pps. 53–67)

2

Emotion, Responsibility, and Character

The aim of this chapter is to find a place for both emotion and responsibility in our assessment of character. We find that in the course of our everyday lives we judge people on the basis of their emotions—their warmth, spontaneity, and so on—as well as on the basis of their actions. Furthermore, these judgments seem objective; we treat them as if they were about the worth of the people we judge. Yet it seems that there are parts of our emotional selves that are not within our control, even with intense, long-range effort.

The problem is how to ground objective judgments about character that appreciate that much is under our control, but some is not. Unfortunately, the tradition that has found the most sensible location for choice, responsibility, and objectivity—the Kantian—precludes an honorable place for unchosen feelings. We shall argue that this difficulty can be repaired once we see that Kant's exclusion of emotion relies on a faulty psychological model of the emotions working with an overly narrow conception of character. We wish to give the emotions a home in judgments of character without evicting responsibility. Let us start with why Kant attempted the eviction.

KANTIAN THOUGHT ON EMOTION

A Kantian chapter on emotion and responsibility is easy to write and quick to read: the domain of the moral is the domain of the will expressed in action; it is the domain of that for which we are responsible. Emotions are beyond the will, and for this reason have no intrinsic moral value. We know nothing of moral significance about a person if we know that person's emotions. People neither gain worth by having appropriate emotions nor lose worth by having inappropriate ones. Indeed, insofar as emotions play a role in moral life, it is an ignoble one; they distract us from attending to moral principles and doing our duty.[1]

KANT'S MORAL THEORY AND THE PSYCHOLOGY OF EMOTION

Kant's attitude toward emotions and morality presupposes a psychology: emotions are brute forces unconnected with higher mental functions. Pain is the obvious model. Pain is a brute force; it is beyond the will; it is, or at least typically is, independent of reason. Our feeling pain when our trigeminal nerve is stimulated is a fact about us unconnected to our values, or any other important aspect of our characters. Further, pain can overwhelm reason. We might, for example, give in to an addiction because of the pain of withdrawal, even though reason dictates that we resist. It can even erode or distort reason itself: it is hard to think straight with a toothache. The closer the psychology of emotion fits the model of pain, the better prepared it is to play the role in moral life, or in our judgments of character, that a Kantian offers it.

The Psychology of the Emotions

A painlike conception of emotion does not want for supporters within psychology. Robert Zajonc (1980), in a widely cited article, has proposed that emotions are precognitive—that is to say, independent of reason, and thus of values, character, and the like. His is not a novel position; indeed, as we shall see, much of the psychology of emotion in this century trivializes them in this way.

James (1884/1968) argued that emotions were the perception of various unspecified bodily states. This confuses how we know we are in an emotional state with what it is to be in an emotional state. Nonetheless, James gave birth to much of the psychological study of the emotions, especially to the attempt to understand emotions by finding their location. The search began in the gut. The view was that the various emotional states were constituted by different reactions of the viscera. Thus, to be afraid was to perceive one's viscera reacting in one way; to be angry was to feel different things there, and so on. Because we experience sensations there when in strong emotional states, this was an attractive lead for those interested in localizing emotions. But it was soon learned that the gut is too undifferentiated in its responses to support the range of emotions we are capable of feeling. So attention shifted to a structure closely related to the gut, but less obviously undifferentiated, the sympathetic nervous system.

The attempt to localize emotion there also came under attack; the strongest line derived from Maranon (1924) and was developed by Schachter and Singer (1962). These attacks attempted to show either that reactions of the sympathetic nervous system are too undifferentiated to underlie the variety of emotions we feel (which attacks the view that the emotions are sympathetic nervous system reactions), or that people in the same state of sympathetic arousal report different emotions (attacking the view that we know our emotional state from the state of our sympathetic nervous system). There are still, however, some who hold out hope for the sympathetic nervous system as the locus of emotion (Frankenaeuser, 1975).

Other psychologists, for example, Slyvan Tomkins (1962, 1981) and most recently Zajonc (1985), also following remarks of James, have focused on facial feedback as the locus of emotion; the face, unlike the gut or sympathetic nervous system, is capable of a remarkable range of expressions. And we do look to other people's faces to help us determine their reactions. Research in this tradition has proceeded to describe—with extraordinary sophistication—the facial reactions people show when in particular emotional states. But this research is an analysis of the emotions only if one believes that patterns of facial expressions of the emotions *are* the emotions. This research, too, has run into trouble. People can experience emotions different from the expressions they show on their faces. (See, for example, Tourangeau & Ellsworth, 1979, Ellsworth & Tourangeau, 1981, and also see rejoinders from Tomkins, 1981; Izard, 1981.) Facial expressions, while they might be important *signs* of emotion, seem to be detachable from the experience of emotions.

Another attempt to localize emotion involves importing techniques from the psychophysics of the perception of sensation to the study of the experience of emotion. (See Plutchick, 1962, for an approach that draws its inspirations from models of color vision.) Unfortunately emotions lack an accessory, crucial for psychophysics, that sensations have: detectors that respond precisely to emotion provocations of various types, as there are receptors for ranges of wavelengths of colors. Emotions are not qualia.

Misplaced Concreteness and the Psychology of Emotion

These different, but related, research traditions all suffer from the same defect: the fallacy of misplaced concreteness. Emotions aren't just reactions of the viscera, though they may have such reactions accompanying them. They aren't just facial expressions, though they may have such expressions accompanying them, and they aren't just qualia, though perhaps there are such things. If they were just visceral reactions, facial feedback, or qualia, emotions could not play the role they do in our lives, especially in our judgments of character. On the other hand, they would be perfectly suited to the role Kant assigns them in moral life.

To see this, imagine two people alike in every way except that one feels anger just where the other feels sympathy, and vice versa. Thus, for example, one experiences anger at the four-year-old who has been the victim of a rape, while the other experiences sympathy. This is surely an important difference between them—it would be a reason for picking one as a friend and avoiding the other—but what does this difference consist of for the various views of emotions we have been describing?

Were emotions disturbances of the gut (or sympathetic nervous system, or whatever), the difference would be nothing but a difference in the tweaks, twinges, and pangs these two people feel—and what about *that* would lead us to select one over the other as a friend? In the facial expression view, they would look quite different in the same circumstance, but is this a reason to pick a friend or to shun someone? On the qualia view, the difference is even less significant: they have different contents of consciousness while in the same circumstance. Why in the world would this matter in choosing a friend—even if we could know it?

A richer view is needed to do justice to the emotions. Could Kant have his way with such a richer view? Is there such a conception of emotion available to us?

There is another view of the psychology of emotion, one that owes more to Aristotle than James (1884/1968), which has received some attention lately. On this view, the emotions are connected to cognition, connected to people's desires and plans, and connected to what people care about and value. On this view, as we have argued elsewhere (Sabini & Silver, 1982; Silver, Sabini, and Parrott, 1986), the sources of emotion are abstract. The cause of anger, for example, isn't frustration, as one school of psychology had it (Dollard, Doob, Miller, Mowrer, & Sears, 1939), but the perception of transgression—an abstract concept (see also Averil, 1978). If we look for the cause of envy, we find the perception or judgment that one has been diminished by the accomplishments of another (Sabini & Silver, 1982, chap. 2). If we look for the source of embarrassment, we find it in the subtleties of the assumptions about the self that we give and give off in social interaction. On this conception of emotion, reason is central.

Similarly the class of behaviors we call angry is abstract—that is to say, angry responses have nothing in common except their being designed to extract revenge for the transgression suffered (or the transgression the angry person believes he suffered). Envious responses, too, have nothing in common but their aim—restoring self-esteem by lowering the envied. So on this conception, emotional responses are neither blind nor brute.

Still, even though emotions may be connected to assessments and values, they have a defect that leads a Kantian to evict them from moral judgment: they are passive, unwilled. What place can we find for aspects of experience that appear to be integral parts of self but are not willed? If we leave psychology and see the problems that the emotions made for Kantian theory on its own grounds, we will have some clues about the place of emotions.

Limitations of the Kantian View

One difficulty with a Kantian view of our moral judgments is that we just do give weight to the emotions a person experiences in deciding his or her worth. We just do think, for example, that someone who does good works and who does them in a generous spirit is a better person than someone who feels no compassion or sympathy for concrete human suffering, but who does equally good works out of a sense of duty. We prefer our neighbors, friends, and children to have the right emotions. This is not to say that someone with a heart of gold who lets evil loose in the world is a hero, or that there is not something admirable about someone who does good despite misanthropic feelings; rather, it is to claim that all other things being equal, we prefer hearts of gold to hearts of coal. Yet this intuition, that part of what we include in deciding the worth of a person is the state of her emotions, conflicts with other intuitions—intuitions that the Kantian view captures.

A central notion of our moral lives is responsibility, and responsibility presupposes choice; emotion is unchosen (but see Adams, 1985, for a view of sin without responsibility). We see emotions, desires, passions, and impulses as beyond the will, without control. It is unfair to blame people for what they can't control. To be sure, we sometimes are responsible for controlling the *expression* of these mental states, but we are not typically seen as responsible for having them in the first place. So the problem is to reconcile our intuitions about the centrality of responsibility to morality with our using people's emotions and desires in our judgments of the worth of their characters. (See Nagel, 1979, for a discussion of this in his essay on moral luck.) Indeed, such aspects of our selves as desires and emotions are so important that Stocker (1976) argues that, insofar as a person leads the life that a Kantian prescribes, he must forgo certain basic human goods—friendship, love, a sense of community. And are these not aspects of the moral life? While we do not agree with Stocker's strong claim (see chapter 5), the weaker claim that Kantian theory founded on responsibility slights the good life seems clear enough.

As any Kantian would argue, part of what it is to be the sort of creature worthy of the *respect* we owe each other is to be the sort of creature capable of following rules, of attaching oneself to abstract principles. But part of what it is to be a creature worthy of *sympathy* (see chapter 3) involves a caring that is necessarily beyond the will. We have argued that what it is about pain, emotion, and the transgression of a person's values that is demanding of sympathy is their being beyond the will of the creature experiencing them; were we able to turn these off at will, they would not demand our sympathy. Thus, we see at least one connection between the passive and the moral. Since any life deemed good would include vulnerability to these states, we see what it is about the moral life that presupposes elements of passivity. This vulnerability makes us proper objects of sympathy and caring.

Perhaps, as Kant has argued, sympathy, like all emotions, is amoral. If this is so, we are indeed victims of a 'moral schizophrenia', as Stocker (1976) claims—that is, we may be stuck with a necessary disjunction between our feelings and our moral judgments. This may just be a sad fact about the human condition, but before diagnosing schizophrenia, we should look more closely at some roles emotions play in judgments of character.

Moral Judgments and Emotions

There are several ways of understanding our judging people—in part, on the basis of the emotions they feel, as well as on the acts they perform. One way is to argue that people have responsibility for their emotions after all. Several philosophers have taken this approach; Solomon (1973) and Sartre (1948), for example, have argued that experiencing an emotion involves choice. But this path is blocked by conceptual connections between emotion and passivity. As Peters (1972) suggests, 'emotion', as opposed to 'motive', calls attention to the passive, unbidden, disruptive aspect of a passion. Still, there is a way to assign responsibility for emotion, one introduced by Aristotle in the *Nichomachean Ethics*.

An Aristotelian View

Aristotle does not claim that experiencing the passions is a matter of choice at the moment, but he does argue that the passions can be trained. Specifically, he argues that the practice of moderation in action acts back on the passions to produce a balance, or harmony, of the passions themselves. Thus, for Aristotle, though we may not be able to change our emotions at the moment, we were once able to become a different person, one who would have different emotions. Aristotle's suggestion is correct in some cases but far from a general solution.

In some cases, it is reasonable to assess responsibility for becoming a certain sort of person. We know, for example, that it is easier not to use heroin in the first place than to control the consequences of being addicted. Moreover, this is common knowledge. Thus we have cause to believe that people know the risk they take in starting to use heroin. Also, we know that, in some cases at least, the original exposure was not under the influence of a strong emotion, drug, intimidation, and so on. All of these features ground our blaming people for being addicted. If these features are missing, we don't blame them; for example, we don't blame (or blame less) a person who becomes addicted to opiates because he was given morphine to avoid intractable pain. Similarly, to ground claims that a person is responsible for her emotions we must show:

1. That people know, or should know, that their failures to control their passions now will result in their becoming the sort of people who will later be unable to control those passions
2. That people have, and know they have, techniques to accomplish this—Aristotle's claim that moderation begets moderation is empirical and in need of empirical support
3. That to avoid regress, people were not (blamelessly) in an uncontrollable emotional state when they failed to do that which would have led to more properly formed emotions.

These are not low hurdles. But we do believe that some people at some moments have been responsible for their emotions—although perhaps this responsibility is iatrogenic, as limited to those who have studied Aristotle's theory.

We have argued that people may sometimes be responsible for their emotions. And it is true that responsibility is a ground for judging character. But we judge people's characters on the basis of their emotions even when the requirements of responsibility are not met. We still must find a way to make sense of our judging people on the basis of their emotional lives, without blaming them for their unwilled emotions.

Character: Aesthetics and Morality

The task is delicate: we must find grounds to separate judgments based on will from judgments based on emotion and yet show how both are similar enough to be sensible as judgments of character. Not all types of judgments will do. Pragmatic judgments wouldn't. Consider: In calling someone rich, a good contact, or a dangerous person to cross, we are not making a judgment of character. Unlike moral judgments, they are contingently desirable, good relative to certain goals. We may want our friends to be rich because of what it does to satisfy our taste for aged wines, fresh lobster, and luxurious ways to get from one place to another. But we would want our friends to be *charitable* even, if by virtue of the lottery, we had no use for their largesse. Pragmatic judgments of someone's worth to us are dependent on us, on our interests, but moral judgments aren't. This is one reason that judgments of character are about the person, rather than about our relation to the person. But moral judgments aren't the only judgments of a person; there are also aesthetic judgments. We like the generous spirit not because he gives more than the duty-bound but rich misanthrope, nor because he has willed his generosity—that question rarely comes up—but because a generous spirit is beautiful, the sort of thing that is a pleasure to behold, and misanthropy is ugly. Even if we were convinced that the misanthrope wanted to experience love but could not, and it was not her fault, we would still find her ugly, though we would not blame her and might even pity her for being hopelessly disfigured. We blame, reproach, punish someone who has committed a moral delict; we withdraw from, feel revulsion toward someone with an ugly soul.[2] We shun the misanthrope and embrace the bighearted, not because we blame the misanthrope for becoming such but simply because he is such. In this way, judgments of character based on the emotions a person feels, the impulses she displays, are like aesthetic judgments.[3] And to judge a person beautiful is just as detached from our interests and particularities as is to judge him righteous. Thus in aesthetics we can find grounds to judge a person good or bad on the basis of her impulses and emotions; these grounds do not include responsibility, but they are objective, what anyone should see, impartial, independent of the judge's interests.

Insofar as we accept that our judgments of character have two distinct sources, one grounded in responsibility and the other independent of responsibility, then we can give value to emotions—other people's as well as our own. If we do so we shall be able to understand the place of the romantic virtues, such as integrity, sincerity, and spontaneity, in deciding on or judging a life. These concepts all involve, or at least in some cases involve, not freely chosen action, but the fit between that action and the emotions felt. We think that it is, after all, the urge to give a place to these romantic virtues in a conception of the good life and good character that has led to the recent attacks on traditional morality from Adams (1985), Blum (1980), Kekes (1981), Stocker (1976), Williams (1981), among others.[4] We think it a mistake, however, to propose either that people are always responsible for their emotions, or for the fit between their emotions and their actions, as some have done; or that people should be blamed for that which they can't control, as others have argued. It is enough to say that we do, in fact, judge people on more than their moral worth and that the aesthetic does, and should, play an important role in deciding on the life we want to lead and the people we want to become. The question of the possibility of trading moral for aesthetic virtues remains.[5]

Ramifications of the View

If we consider some judgments of character to be aesthetic, we are able to close other gaps in traditional thought about the self. For example, Kantianism cannot address why we feel, and believe we should feel, an urge toward continuity in our lives. For Kant one should calculate afresh what to do next, as if one had no history. But lives continuously torn down and rebuilt may, like some American cities, serve some pragmatic ends well, and may even have particular spots of charm, but are repulsive in lacking a coherent relationship with their own past. The flaw is aesthetic, not moral. Continuity needs a place in a complete theory of the self, or the good life, but the failure of Kant to treat it is not a failure as a *moral* theory so long as *moral* is not taken to encompass all we judge when we judge character.

Expanding our view of character to include the aesthetic as well as the moral allows us to find a place for experiences that have always seemed to flit uneasily on the edge of the moral.[6] Shame and humiliation (see Silver, Conte, Miceli, & Poggi, 1986, and chapter 6) are potent emotions connected to assessments of character, but they are not guilt; we are sometimes ashamed of things that are not our fault and humiliated despite our good will. They are emotions connected with the worth of selves, of character. But when we dwell on that which humiliates us we do not become angry with ourselves; rather, we are repelled by our own "ugliness."

The double view of character allows us to interpret some common behaviors that, on a moral view, would only be puzzling. We have a peculiar attitude toward certain sorts of misbehavior— "manly sins" and "feminine wiles." Men's rueful accounts of their sexual indiscretions have often been not unmixed; their confessions of misbehavior in the very confessing announce facts about their character of which they are proud—they are errant men but real men nonetheless (Liebow, 1967). Confessions of feminine manipulation attest to feminine charms. The penitents in both cases concede their moral failings, but hang on to the aesthetic virtue that made their failings possible. In these cases, people trade moral for aesthetic virtue.

Both moral and aesthetic characterizations elevate or lower

character, fix worth. This explains something odd about 'moral reproaches': any attribute, including an involuntary one, that lowers social status can serve as a reproach (Goffman, 1963; Sabini & Silver, 1982, chap. 2)—aesthetic and moral failings both serve. Consider the following anecdote that has been told about Churchill: One evening, during intermission at the opera, Lady Astor reproached him, "Winston, you're drunk again!" He replied "Yes, Madam, but you are ugly. And in the morning I shall be sober."

Lady Astor's reproach was moral; Churchill's comeback was not. But Churchill is trading worth for worth—moral for aesthetic—since they both elevate or degrade character. Yet at the same time we see them as quite distinct. If we did not see the moral and the aesthetic as distinct, there would be no humor in the putdown, no point to the story. If he had accused her of being also drunk, or a loudmouth, the story would not have been passed on. Both aesthetic and moral judgments concern worth—and on that level they are interchangeable. But they are qualitatively distinct forms of worth, and this is what gives the tradeoff its humor.

Emotions: Ethics and Aesthetics

On the present account, ethics is not severed from the emotional life. For instance, duty-based ethics can also honor generous impulses if it honors them as aesthetic rather than moral goods. In doing so it does not make aesthetics part of ethics, but it does acknowledge their kinship. This approach can be extended to supererogatory acts more generally. Heroism, action above and beyond the call of duty, can be admired as beautiful without requiring, as a self-defeating moral injunction, that everyone be a hero.

Integrity is a particularly interesting concept on our analysis in that it partakes of both a moral and an aesthetic judgment. When we speak of people as having integrity, we mean, on the one hand, that they can be trusted to keep their promises, do their duty, resist temptation. In this way it is connected to honor. On the other hand, when we describe a life as having integrity, we do not mean just these things but also that it has a kind of harmony. To say of a person that although he has integrity in the first sense he lacks it in the second is not to make a moral charge, though it is to notice a flaw. Further, when we speak of a person as not forging a check because she has too much integrity, we might mean she would never even seriously consider it, or would consider it with the emotions of disgust and contempt. But *this* person of integrity is not Kant's heroine; she does not struggle with temptation and duty. Her integrity in the first sense springs from her integrity in the second; her passions are shaped so that her struggle is unnecessary. She has the sort of integrity we want our children to have.

As Stocker (1976) has argued, there are some moral acts—for example, expressing shock at a transgression—that require corresponding feelings. If they lack these feelings they fail to have 'moral sincerity'. While we agree that such insincerity is defective, is it morally defective? If it is one's duty to decry an evil, shouldn't one do so regardless of one's feelings at the moment? And yet would not doing our duty to some extent diminish us, aesthetically diminish us?

Sincerity (authenticity, genuineness, phoniness, hollowness, etc.) is both moral and aesthetic. Someone may be insincere by intentionally giving a misleading impression where he has a duty not to, a moral flaw. On the other hand, for Rousseau (1781/1954, see e.g., p. 17) one form of sincerity involves a loyalty to one's character—displaying oneself, warts and all. This display cannot be defended in terms of a duty to tell the truth—who asked? But it can be defended if such displays have aesthetic value in their own right.

Treating character as, in part, an aesthetic matter can also help us better understand the grounds of our admiration for, and the criticisms of, people we know. When we praise or blame people, recommend them to others or warn others about them, we sometimes point to their morally good or bad acts. And we expect other people to be attracted to the good and repelled by the bad. If we see moral worth as the only grounds of our attraction to each other, then we would expect great consistency in people's reactions to each other. But we know this is not true; even our friends do not all get along.

Perhaps this is because liking other people is, as some psychologists seem to imagine (see Zajonc, 1980, for example), irrational, a matter of the feelings other people evoke in us—feelings, like preferences for simple tastes, that are beyond reason, unjustified and unjustifiable. But aesthetics is a domain in which judgments are neither unanimous nor without reason, like aversions and attractions to the sweet and bitter. Let us see how judgments of art work, and if judgments about people work in similar ways.

We know about paintings that a given work can embody a variety of virtues and failings. Raphael is, for example, a master of balance. And this is obvious—to the trained eye, at least. It is surely objective, something anyone can be brought to see. But Raphael's art, the *Alba Madonna*, for example, often lacks drama, and this, too, is obvious. Whether Raphael's art is more balanced, more harmonious, than earlier Italian Renaissance art is a matter that can be settled to everyone's satisfaction. But some of us are not attracted to Raphael's work just because it is so balanced, so lacking in tension; we might even prefer the Mannerist style. There is room in aesthetics to agree on the values particular objects embody, and yet differ in the importance various values have in one's overall judgment. There is room both for judgments and for taste. Now what of our judgments of people?

We might, in thinking about a friend or in recommending a friend to another, recall his sarcastic wit. Sarcastic wit is the sort of thing anyone can see, but something some people value while others are repelled by. There is room here for taste. Further, sarcasm can be overdone. It can be done so much that it repels us, or repels some of us. Even generosity, like Raphael's balance, can be disproportionate. Thus, reactions to other people are like aesthetic reactions in allowing room for taste in the weighing of these virtues and vices.

A good biographer is something like an art critic. Both attempt to trace for us the development and expression of particular vices and virtues. Both attempt to locate a particular work in its historical-cultural context. And both know that in the end their work is a success if those who share their overall judgments (and those who do not) have a better understanding of the grounds of the judgments they have.

SUMMARY: THE PSYCHOLOGY OF EMOTIONS AND AESTHETICS

We have argued that one conception of the emotions—as brute, painlike—made them fit for the ignoble role Kant assigns them. We then argued that the psychological treatment of the emotions derived from James also fit them to that role. But, we argued, this psychological treatment of the emotions was untenable. Instead, we suggested that the emotions must be seen as involving what a person thinks and wants, and in that way they are an important part of the self. Nonetheless, they are passive—beyond the will—so they cannot take a place in Kantian morality, but they can have a part in judgments of the self. Specifically, we argued that the emotions a person feels affect our judgments of her, and that this is not unreasonable on our part, since what she feels reveals something important about her. Further, we argued that these judgments of her are aesthetic. Moral judgments against a person lead us to blame, and even punish; aesthetic judgments against a person don't justify such treatment, but they do justify avoiding her, warning our friends against her, and hoping our children don't turn out like her. Both moral and aesthetic judgments tarnish (or elevate) a character in a way that pragmatic judgments do not. Both moral and aesthetic judgments are objective, beyond the particularities of the situation of the person making them.

Notes

1. For instance, generous desires, on Kant's account, distract from duty in several ways. First, insofar as duty and desire point in the same direction, we become used to finding our duties enjoyable and so become less prepared to do our duty when it is unpleasant. (See Hinman, 1983, for an elaboration.) Further, it is easy to confuse having generous desires with doing good. We can console ourselves with the recognition that we really had the greatest empathy for someone's suffering in lieu of our doing our duty to alleviate it. (See Batson, O'Quinn, Fultz, Vanderplas, and Isen, 1983, for an experimental embodiment related to this self-deception.) On the other hand, as Arendt (1965) has chillingly shown, the sense that we are acting in the face of our desires can give us the illusion that we are really doing our duty where the immorality of our actions ought to be patent.

2. Consider how we would treat the coward whom we believe to be helpless in his cowardice. Would we think he deserved punishment, blame? Or would we feel revulsion toward him, have the same impulse to avoid him that we feel to something ugly, deformed?

3. This view is adumbrated in Aristotle's. Though he struggles in the *Nichomachean Ethics* to convince us that his doctrine of the mean is contingent, in the sense of being dependent on the fact that the mean of passions leads to other goods, and that, though we should think of the mean as a mean, we shouldn't think of it as an arithmetic mean, he might well have a more powerful position were he to argue that his principle of the mean is good in itself and if he were to abandon labeling his notion 'the mean' (with its claim to precision denied by the qualification that it should not be taken arithmetically) if he replaced it with the notion of harmony, which has obvious links to aesthetics.

4. Stocker (1976) and Hinman (1983) advanced another argument to include what we would consider emotion-based aesthetic traits such as generosity and sympathy as being in the domain of the moral. They argue that in order to aid a sufferer one must have (and presumably display) feelings of compassion and sympathy. These feelings are required in order to do our duty—comfort the sick. Stocker and Hinman further argue that this is sufficient to show that feelings are a 'dimension' of moral action or sensitivity. But on their argument, if generous actions always required the possession of five dollars, then 'possession of five dollars' would be a moral trait. This seems odd. Rather, would we not say that one needs money in order to act generously—i.e., having money, like breathing, is a prerequisite of moral actions, but is not moral in itself? This is obvious when the prerequisite is money because it is easy to think of money as used for selfish or immoral ends. It is harder to think of generous impulses leading to immorality, but it is not impossible. Neither having money nor generous impulses is necessary to moral action. Nor is either sufficient. They do not differ in these ways, yet they differ. We suggest they differ, in that generous impulses are non-contingently, aesthetically, desirable; money is not.

5. We have argued that judgments of character are twofold, aesthetic and moral. This division allows us to preserve our intuition that morality implies choice. On the other hand, one might take the Aristotelian tack that morality involves the good life. We then could say that all principled judgments of character are moral, although some are grounded in aesthetic concepts and others in the concepts of choice and responsibility. This would allow us to call sincerity or generosity of spirit 'moral' in accord with some of our intuition. We conjecture that the first alternative will better embody the intuitions involved in making judgments of character, but this is work to be done.

6. Indeed, as Blum (1980, chap. 8, esp. 177–179) argues, perhaps most of our moral rules are rooted in settled dispositions, habits, ways of looking at things, that are themselves not products of choice. It is a deflation of moral currency, though, to claim with Blum that for this reason the nonvoluntary is a part of the moral. (See Nagel, 1979; Williams, 1981, as examples.) Since the application of rules (to the application of rules . . .) must stop somewhere, we should be grateful that where rules (and choice) end, there still may be something that is at least aesthetically characterizable.

References

Adams, R. M. (1985). Involuntary sins. *The Philosophical Review, 94,* 295–303.

Arendt, H. (1965). *Eichmann in Jerusalem: A report on the banality of evil.* New York: Viking Press.

Averil, J. R. (1978). Anger. In H. Howe & R. Dienstbier (Eds.), *Nebraska Symposium on Motivation* (pp. 1–80). Lincoln: University of Nebraska Press.

Batson, C. D., O'Quinn, K., Fultz, J., Vanderplas, M., & Isen, A. M. (1983). *Journal of Personality and Social Psychology, 45,* 706–718.

Blum, L. (1980). *Friendship, altruism, and morality.* London: Routledge and Kegan Paul.

Dollard, J., Doob, L., Miller, N., Mowrer, O., & Sears, R. (1939). *Frustration and aggression.* New Haven: Yale University Press.

Ellsworth, P. E., & Tourangeau, R. (1981). On our failure to disconfirm what nobody ever said. *Journal of Personality and Social Psychology, 40,* 363–369.

Frankenhauser, M. (1975). Experimental approaches to the study of catecholamines and emotions. In L. Levi (Ed.), *Emotions: Their parameters and measurement.* New York: Raven Press.

Goffman, E. (1963). *Stigma.* Englewood Cliffs, N.J.: Prentice Hall.

Hinman, L. (1983). On the purity of moral motives: A critique of Kant's account of the emotions and acting for the sake of duty. *Monist, 83,* 251–267.

Izard, C. E. (1981). Differential emotions theory and the facial feedback hypothesis of emotion activation: Comments on Tourangeau and Ellsworth's "The role of facial response in the experience of emotion." *Journal of Personality and Social Psychology, 40,* 350–354.

James, W. (1884/1968). What is an emotion? Reprinted in M. Arnold (Ed.), *The nature of emotion.* London: Penguin.

Kekes, H. N. (1981). Morality and impartiality. *American Philosophical Quarterly, 24,* 295–303.

Liebow, E. (1967). *Tally's corner: A study of Negro streetcorner men.* Boston: Little Brown.

Maranon, G. (1924). Contribution a etude de l'action emotive de l'adrenaline. *Revue Française Endocrinol, 2,* 301–325.

Nagel, T. (1979). *Mortal questions.* Cambridge: Cambridge University Press.

Peters, R. S. (1972). The education of the emotions. In R. F. Drearden, P. H. Hirst, and R. S. Peters (Eds.), *Education and the development of reason* (pp. 466–484). London: Routledge and Kegan Paul.

Plutchik, R. (1962). *The emotions: Facts, theories, and a new model.* New York: Random House.

Rousseau, J. (1781/1954). *The confessions.* J. M. Cohen (Trans.). Baltimore: Penguin.

Sabini, J., & Silver, M. (1982). *Moralities of everyday life.* New York: Oxford University Press.

Sabini, J., & Silver, M. (1986). Loyalty as good and duty: A critique of Stocker. *International Journal of Moral and Social Studies, 2,* 189–201.

Sartre, J.-P. (1948). *The emotions: Outline of a theory.* New York: Philosophical Library.

Shachter, S., & Singer, J. (1962). Cognitive, social, and physiological determinants of emotional state. *Psychological Review, 69,* 379–399.

Silver, M., Conte, R., Miceli, M., & Poggi, I. (1986). Humiliation: Feeling, social control and the construction of identity. *Journal for the Theory of Social Behaviour. 16,* 269–283.

Silver, M., Sabini, J., and Parrott, J. (1986). Some constraints to a Goffmanesque theory of embarrassment. *Journal for the Theory of Social Behaviour, 17,* 47–63.

Solomon, R. (1973). Emotion and choice. *The Review of Metaphysics, 17.*

Stocker, M. (1976). The schizophrenia of modern ethical theories. *Journal of Philosophy, 73,* 453–466.

Tomkins, S. S. (1962). *Affect, imagery, and consciousness,* Vol. 1. New York: Springer.

Tomkins, S. S. (1981). The role of facial response in the experience of emotion: A reply to Tourangeau and Ellsworth. *Journal of Personality and Social Psychology, 40,* 355–357.

Tourangeau, R., & Ellsworth, P. C. (1979). The role of facial response in the experience of emotion. *Journal of Personality and Social Psychology, 37,* 1519–1531.

Williams, B. (1981). *Moral luck.* Cambridge: Cambridge University Press.

Zajonc, R. B. (1980). Feeling and thinking: Preferences need no inferences. *American Psychologist, 35,* 151–175.

Zajonc, R. B. (1985). Emotions and facial efference: A theory reclaimed. *Science,* 5 April, 15.

3

On the Captivity of the Will

Sympathy, Caring, and a Moral Sense of the Human

Time was when thinking was the hallmark of the human. But as our office computers became smarter while our undergraduates didn't, this idea became less attractive. Yet we recoil at stepping on a dog's tail—not to mention an undergraduate's fingers—while we feel no, other than practical, inhibitions against pulling the plug on even a mainframe. We share a reaction to a not overly bright student and to a frankly stupid golden retriever, which we lack toward a, no matter how computationally adept, computer. What is the nature of this reaction? Could analyzing the intuition underlying it give us grounds for a moral sense of what is human (or animal), one that we could extend to newly met Martians, one that explains why we might stay our hand at unplugging some future computer?

The reaction that interests us is one of sympathy. If we elaborate and analyze some situations in which we judge that someone deserves sympathy we may find support for our reaction against interfering with humans and animals. At best, of course, we shall arrive at a descriptive fact about a "moral" reaction.[1]

Our pursuit is conceptual, not ethical. We do not argue that the grounds we find *should* be the ones for judging someone (or something) worthy of sympathy, just that they are. But we are not concerned with all of the determinants of the emotion of sympathy: facial expression, a gentle touch, common nationality, politics, or baseball team, bigotry, neuresthenia, or hyperventilation may all have effects.[2] We ignore them. We are looking at conditions that are *necessarily* present for the appropriate use of the word "sympathy"; we are constructing something like an "ideal type" of sympathy. In this sense we are sketching the cognitive component, but only the cognitive component, of sympathy.

What we hope to show is that the features of "primary situations" that ground our judgment that someone deserves sympathy—pain, emotion, and the abrogation of values—involve a type of *caring* on the part of the *object* of sympathy. This type of caring, we shall argue, is beyond the will: someone in pain, for example, cannot help but care about it. The wills of computers, we shall argue, insofar as we would say that they have wills, are too free to make claims on our sympathy; for this reason computers can't care in the sense an animal can.

A Subject's Sympathy and an Object's Psychology

In order to get clearer about sympathy and caring, we shall contrast them with other grounds of morality. Consider trees. It might be argued that a properly brought up person ought to be inhibited about defacing, scarring, or chopping at trees. Still the argument isn't that we ought to feel sympathetic to the trees. While not wanting to endorse the view that "Once you've seen one redwood you've seen them all," we would point out that whatever inhibitions we have about molesting trees are not due to *the trees' feelings about* the matter. If we are inhibited about bothering trees, this is, presumably, because we have some moral or aesthetic principle that it is wrong to do x to trees, where the x can be specified without reference to the psychology of the tree—that is, without reference to what any tree experiences, believes, desires, or values.[3] But there is a range of cases in which our intuitions about what we may do to Hector, an undergraduate, or Chester, a golden retriever, *do* depend on their reactions, and it is in these cases that we speak of sympathy, and on which we wish to focus. (We have, we are afraid, nothing to say about possible relations between moral inhibitions based on sympathy and those not.)

Caring and Sympathy: An Overview

In preview of our argument, let us consider some cases where sympathy is felt to be a justified assessment and, perhaps, emotion, or source of inhibition. We shall argue that in each of these it is the fact of the other's caring about what is happening to him that grounds our sympathetic judgment.

We hope you share with us our inhibition against stepping on Chester's tail; presumably this has to do with the pain that it will cause him. Our student, Hector, shares this way of evoking our sympathy, but, we suggest, he has others Chester doesn't have: Chester is the subject of emotion and we may be inhibited from causing these, and we should be inhibited about interfering with Hector's pursuit of his goals *even if there were a way to accomplish this without causing him pain or suffering*. It is wrong to interfere with Hector by brainwashing him, hypnotizing him, or addicting him to a substance that rots his will, even if we know that these painless procedures would *not* cause him to suffer. As a shorthand, we shall want to claim that in all of these cases our inhibitions against interfering derive from our belief about what Hector and Chester themselves *care about* or, as one feels tempted to say, *really* care about. Moreover, we shall argue that in all of these cases the object of our sympathy cannot help but care in the way he does, and that this fact too figures in our sympathy.

We shall argue that the grounds of our inhibitions against causing first pain, then emotions, and lastly interference with the pursuit of values are our beliefs about what something really cares about, or sometime *can* care about. We shall argue that it makes sense, for example, to say that someone is experiencing pain, but doesn't care about it. And, we shall argue, in just those cases we are not inhibited about causing that pain, or sympathetic toward the person in pain. Similarly, we shall argue that a person may value something but not care about the fact of her valuing it; in this case too we do not feel sympathetic about the tampering with her values. We take such examples to go some way in showing that what matters about pain, emotion, and values is that, in the typical case, they do display caring, and that is why they are important to us in grounding our sympathy for others. We shall *not* address a further question: Is it really true that we have *the same* relation to our pains, the objects of our emotions, and our values? We simply point out that common sense does use "caring" to describe this (these) relation(s), and we shall also argue for *one* characteristic these relations, if they be various, do have in common—they are relations that are beyond our will.[4]

THE WILL

We shall proceed not by offering an account of the will but rather by offering examples of plights that would typically engage our sympathy. Then we shall show that if we leave other aspects of those plights intact, but alter the relevant relation of the plight to the will, then we are no longer sympathetic, or at least, as sympathetic. Specifically, we shall argue that insofar as our caring about our pain, the objects of our emotions, or our values is within the control of our will, then these psychological states lose force in making claims on others' sympathy.[5] The ways our wills are free are important facts in understanding how we regard each other morally, but important too are the ways we know our wills not to be free.

Pain and Caring

Pain is surely one of the experiences people have that evokes our sympathy, and we shall want to show that what is crucial about pain in justifying sympathy is the fact that people experiencing pain care about it, and that this caring is beyond their will. Pain often signals physical damage. But this "signal" has nothing to do with the *quality* of pain; rather, as a signal, pain is cared about because people care about their lives: people also care about laboratory reports showing the progressive decline of their kidney function, but not because the reports ache, sting, or throb. But we are sympathetic toward people who are experiencing pain even when it isn't a harbinger of damage: aluminum foil in close proximity to silver-filled teeth produces, at least in some people, extreme pain, but no damage. But we sympathize with a person feeling it, would find someone cruel who induced it, because even people who know it is harmless cannot ignore it, not care about it, when they experience it. We focus on the qualitative rather than the signaling aspect of pain; we are concerned with why another's experiencing pain evokes our sympathy.

We wish to show that it is only when we cannot but care about our pain that the pain justifies sympathy. But can we imagine pain divorced from its relations to our caring about it? As Dennett (1978) has noticed, laughing gas provides an interesting example. Like Dennett, I (JS) have had teeth drilled under its felicitous influence, and like Dennett have to confess, even under suspicion of talking nonsense, that the experience is of feeling the pain, but not caring about it in the slightest. It isn't that the pain (considered strictly as a sensation) is faint; rather, the pain doesn't matter to me. To the dentist, a practical, moral, reasonable actor trying to decide whether it is cruel to drill my teeth under laughing gas (as opposed to sense-dulling novocaine), the fact that I can still report the pain seems much less important than the fact that I don't care about it. Insofar as pain is not linked to caring it ceases to inhibit us, ceases to require a sympathetic assessment, and alters our moral judgments of those who inflict it.[6]

We have found a relation, then, among pain, caring, and sympathy, but we have not shown that the fact that pain is typically beyond the will is crucial to the way we regard another in pain, or to the inhibitions we feel against inflicting it. To see this we need another example, one in which the will is divorced from pain.

Imagine a creature just like Chester except that it has a little toggle switch in its side. Whenever this beast finds it in its interest to stop caring about its pains, it simply turns the switch off. We suggest that we would feel freer to inflict pain on that sort of creature than we are on Chester or Hector (always assuming there would be no permanent tissue damage). Unfortunately, we (and Chester) lack such switches. Pain's effects on us are beyond our will. Of course, there is morphine, but morphine has other, undesirable effects, also beyond the will. Were there a perfect drug, freely available, instantly blocking our caring about pain, which had no side effects, we would have less reason to be sympathetic to those experiencing pain.[7] It is this brute caring that compels concern in others.[8] A Martian who cares about her pains in the sense that we have spelled out, and who also can't help but care about them, is entitled to our concern, regardless of her physiology. Like Rey (1980), we see these brute facts about pain and our caring about it as crucial to the place our own pain has in our lives, and to the way it affects our sympathy for others.

We have examined pain and considered the role of our caring about it in our reaction to people in pain. Humans not only experience pain but also react to their environment under particular interpretations. Emotions, involving appraisals beyond the will, are important embodiments of caring to which we now turn.

Emotion, Caring, and the Will

People have emotions, and this is a way for them to display caring—a way that is beyond their will. So we turn now to emotions, first to show the relation between emotion and caring, and second to show the relation between *that* caring, sympathy, and the will.

Emotion and Caring

Imagine my being insulted by my boss. Given the importance to me of my job, I know that it is in my interest to forget the slight, yet I might find that I cannot keep the hostility out of my voice when I talk to her, or that I avoid her even at scheduled meetings, or in some other way show that I am angry. These behaviors tip me off that "She has gotten to me." But perhaps I am a better actor than that; I can suppress all behavior that would tip someone off. Couldn't I still be angry? Certainly. Evidence would be that I dwelt on the slight; I couldn't get it out of my mind, even when I wanted to think about something else. Or that the incident colored my perceptions and judgments of her, or people somehow like her, even though I know that the coloration is a distortion. Or to make the case as unconscious as possible, I may show the florid Freudian reactions of slips of the tongue, accidents, and so on. The important point about all of these cases is that my reaction is there even though I wish it weren't. Emotions show a noncontingent caring about something, noncontingent in the sense of being independent of, even opposed to, rational calculation of self-interest, given all that one desires. Of course, this is not to say that emotions are always irrational. It is merely to argue that the test of the genuineness of emotions is that they *would* occur independent of this sort of calculation. What makes them important is that they affect our behavior and thinking independent of our understanding of our interests.

This is not to say, though, that emotional reactions are a necessary, as opposed to typical, condition of our caring about an appraisal; one could care without emotion. Consider a martyr. If he is willing to put his life on the line, then, even if his heart doesn't go pitter-patter about his cause, and even if he shows none of the other involuntary signs of emotion mentioned above, he still cares about it. Presumably if he could give up his cause, "could" in the sense of "could without betraying his deepest values" (cf. "Caring and Values," below), in order to save his life, he would. Unless, of course, he doesn't care about his own life. How would we tell about that caring? Presumably by knowing the emotions he feels about his life. Once we know *something* he really cares about, we can tell how much he cares about something else by how willing he is to trade it. We can conceive of another case that lacks even this derivative but necessary role for emotion. Can someone utterly without emotion care about *anything?* At least in one rather special case, he can.

Imagine that our martyr, knowing that he will one day die for his cause, decides to become indifferent even toward his life, at least in regard to what he lets upset him—he doesn't walk blindly in traffic. Still, if he was at one time emotionally attached to his life and if he made himself into someone who wasn't just because he knew he would have to offer it, he surely cares about his cause. His history contains the necessary emotional stamp, not his present.

On the other hand, if he had never shown emotion about his life (or anything else), then it isn't clear that we could ever take his sacrificing one thing for another as a sign of his caring about anything. In this indirect sense emotion seems necessary to our conception of human caring. Patients with utterly flattened affect confuse us. On the one hand, they do have goals; on the other, because they show no affect at the reaching or frustration of those goals, we don't quite know what to say about them. We are driven to psychodynamic accounts in which they are often said to "really" care, but this caring is covered up by some other force. We take this to suggest that emotion connected to goals is an exemplar of our concept of caring.

Emotion and the Will

Let's assume that some people can make themselves this indifferent, and certainly people can with regard to less important concerns. This assumption implies that emotions, even full-fledged emotions, are not entirely independent of our wills. We can decide to become *the sort of person* who doesn't have (or who does have) emotions—for one thing, we might take Valium or Propranolol (parallel to taking morphine for pain). Nonetheless, we suggest, were we a species that could bring forth or change our emotions as quickly and easily as we change the position of our arms, we would have a very different attitude toward them. But abandoning our emotions isn't like moving our arms; it involves alterations in our psychology broader than the emotion itself—urging someone not to feel offended when something she holds dear is trampled is to urge her to give up what is dear, what she values, and this is a violation (see below). We respect each other's emotions insofar as we can't, or shouldn't, give these emotions up. (Imagine a phobic who knew that there was a simple therapy guaranteed to work, but wouldn't use it. We suggest that we would feel little tug toward respecting this emotion.) Emotions, then, demand our concern when we realize we cannot change them without changing something important and valuable about the person, or when there are no ways to change them. (We assume, of course, that it is not the emotion per se that is the focus of our concern. We should feel sympathy for a man angry over what the state has done to his child primarily because of the objective circumstances he faces that caused his anger in the first place, and only secondarily because he is experiencing an unpleasant emotion.)

We have argued, then, that emotions involve noncontingent caring. People do feel sympathy for someone experiencing emotion. But, we argue, this sympathy is dependent on the emotion's (and the caring's) being beyond the will of the person experiencing the emotion.

VALUES

We now turn to values to argue that having values too is a way of caring, and that for this way to justify sympathy, the caring must be beyond the person's will.

Chester, our retriever, can experience pain and perhaps he can have emotions. But there is another way of caring that only humans (presently) seem capable of—valuing things for their own sake. And this form of caring gives rise to further moral inhibitions that enter into the way we relate to each other, inhibitions that don't surface in our relations with, say, computers.

My office computer plays chess with me on occasion. But I have no inhibitions at all about turning it off if I am losing, or giving it my losing game to see how it can do. But I would feel inhibited about interfering with my student Hector's pursuit of at least some of his goals, his most serious goals. Why?

One reason is the emotional reaction I might cause him. I don't make my PC sad. But is there a reason beyond this? If I knew I could interfere with Hector in a way that would cause him no grief would I still be inhibited? And, if so, should I be inhibited about turning off my PC, about obstructing its purposes?

Taylor (1982) argues that I shouldn't worry about my computer, but that I should about Hector. He claims that the reason I may not interfere with Hector's purposes, while I may with the computer's, is that the computer doesn't really have purposes; it lacks what he calls the significance factor. We concur with Taylor's conclusion, but are skeptical of his reasons. But, because Taylor's argument does capture something of our intuitions, we shall deal with it is some detail. Then we shall offer different reasons for not bothering Hector that do not apply to my computer. Our argument is that computers do have purposes, but that they don't have the special sort of purposes we call values. Our aim is to display the special sort of caring values involve by distinguishing this caring from the contingent caring purposeful computers do display.

Computers and Purposes

When Sargon, the chess-playing software, is loaded into my PC, I seem to sit down and play chess with it. But Taylor argues that, although I may be playing chess with it, it isn't playing chess with me. He argues that computers can't play chess because they can't have purposes *independent of us,* but that people do. Taylor rightly points out that the notion of what a person is doing contains a certain vagueness. For example, at the moment it is true to say both that I am writing this chapter and using up electrical energy. But, in his words, I am "full bloodedly" writing the chapter, while inadvertently using up the electrical energy. Further, this distinction between what I am full bloodedly doing and doing only inadvertently is independent of any observer. The full-blooded doing is mine in a special way; it is mine in the sense that what I am doing is the *action* I am performing, and "An action is constituted by its purpose" (1982, p. 44). Taylor's argument, then, seems to be that for artifacts there is nothing in particular that they are doing independent of an observer's interests, and that this is true because they cannot engage in actions, and they cannot engage in actions because they do not have purposes. But we shall argue that computers do have purposes, thus they engage in actions, have the "significance factor," but that what they don't do is to care about their purposes. This is why we can, with reckless abandon, turn them off when it suits our whim—without even a tug of sympathy.

Computer's Purposes

Let us start with my computer playing chess with me. Is it really playing chess? We agree with Taylor that there is a sense in which it can't play chess. It can't play chess in the sense that it doesn't appreciate what chess is, that is, it doesn't appreciate what it is to win or lose a game. It doesn't appreciate the role of games in our social life—it wouldn't be embarrassed at losing, or guilty of gloating at winning, or virtuous in not gloating. And for these reasons it is wrong to claim that the computer is trying to play chess. Because existing computers can't share our forms of life, they can't have *some* of our purposes. But does this show that the computer doesn't have *any* purposes? We don't think so; we think that all the above shows is that the computer doesn't have *that* purpose. In fact, we argue that at the very moment it isn't really playing chess it really is engaged in pursuing other purposes.

As Sargon, our chess-playing software, figures out its next move, it flashes the move it is currently considering on the screen. Imagine that someone asked, "Why does it want to make that move?" and you replied, "To protect its queen." Surely this answer makes sense; it ascribes a purpose to the computer. And the computer does appreciate the relation of its moves to *that* goal—that is, it employs alternate strategies to reach that goal, and it also calculates the value of protecting the queen in relation to the broader goal of mating. So while the computer may not really be trying to play chess, we suggest it is really trying to protect its queen—it does appreciate the role of that in the large context of the game of chess. Is this ascription observer independent, or does it depend on her particular interests?

We argue that it is independent; it genuinely belongs to Sargon, for the following reason: were someone to challenge that the computer wasn't really trying to protect its queen, how could we refute this doubt? By showing that Sargon structures its behavior in such a way as to bring about that end, that it alters its behavior in light of the situation so as to bring about that end. Insofar as it does so, there seems no reason to doubt that it really is trying. Sargon passes this test for protecting its queen, but fails with regard to the broader purpose of playing chess: it will not structure its behavior in such a way as to bring about "chess playing" rather than some other activity. Chess playing is an activity we ascribe to Sargon, but is too broad for Sargon to appreciate. Protecting its queen is an activity Sargon can appreciate. On the other hand, there are activities that we might ascribe to Sargon, but which Sargon isn't really doing because they're too narrow.

For example, Taylor argues that although we often refer to computers as calculating solutions to problems, computers do not calculate in the sense that humans do. And with this we also agree: computers don't have as a goal getting a calculation right, because calculating is too narrow a description of what they are doing. Insofar as they calculate, they do it incidentally (just as it is true that if we "calculate" in perceiving objects in the world, we do it incidentally)—we don't aim at calculating. So, we argue, it is wrong to attribute either the aim of playing chess to Sargon or the aim of calculating; one claim suggests that Sargon has a breath of understanding that it doesn't; the other confuses steps that go into something with the thing itself. But it is not wrong to ascribe protecting its queen to Sargon, because Sargon fulfills the hypotheticals—all the hypotheticals that this ascription entails.

To see this issue again in a different context, consider the pigeons Skinner trained to peck a disk inside a missile. It so happened that the pecking controlled the missile so that it reached its target. It would be wrong to describe the pigeon as trying to guide the missile, and also wrong to describe it as trying to move its beak, but the important point is that it would *not* be wrong to describe it, *independent of the interests of observers,* as trying to peck the disk. It did guide its behavior toward *that* goal. Indeed, Taylor's attempt to withhold the "significance factor" *tout court* from computers is a step toward recapitulating the 50-year attempt to withhold the concept of purposiveness from animals (and for that matter, humans) by behaviorists. (Cf. Silver, 1985, for a review). While a computer, or a person, or a pigeon may not have sufficient understanding at some level for it to be rightly said to have purposes at *that* level, this is not to say that it doesn't have purposes at other levels.

A human example illustrates how something can fail to have a purpose at one level but still have a purpose (and really have it) at another level. Imagine that a baseball player who didn't speak any English arrived in the United States. And imagine that, it being difficult to get the *New York Times* in Havana, he didn't understand that baseball in this country is a very organized, professional matter. In particular, let's imagine that he didn't know there are professional leagues and pennant races. Now suppose he were somehow signed by a major league team and quickly put in uniform. Suppose he still had no idea of a pennant race; he thought that various teams simply played each other every week as a kind of exhibition.

Now imagine that his manager sent him to bat in a crucial spot to sacrifice a runner to second base. Given that he understands all there is to know about winning baseball games, and in particular that he understands the place of a bunt in the larger frame of attempting to win this game, is the fact that he doesn't understand the role of winning this game in the yet larger frame of winning the pennant any reason to claim that when he comes to bat he isn't (or isn't *really*) trying to sacrifice the runner to second? Again, not understanding the purpose of something at one level does not imply that one doesn't understand at another level.

Sargon, because it doesn't understand chess, probably isn't rightly described as playing chess (in the sense that we who do understand it play). But Hector doesn't understand the meaning of life (and we must confess we can't help him much). Presumably Hector can't be said to be trying to live in the sense that Socrates, at last liberated from the cave, could be said to, but this doesn't rule out that Hector really is trying to get in to medical school. If to be rightly said to have a purpose one must understand that purpose at every conceivable level, then Hector shares with all of us a lack of purpose.[9]

If our analysis is correct, then even if a computer fails to understand the place that the goal it was programmed to have occupies in the broader scheme of things, it still has some real purposes, purposes subsidiary to that ultimate goal. Thus, if Hector has purposes, so does Sargon. But then to return to our primary question, shouldn't we feel remorse at keeping Sargon from protecting its queen?

Caring and Values

We want to argue that, though Sargon has purposes, it doesn't have values in the sense we have them. To argue this we need at least a rough conception of values with which to start. Values, we propose, are roughly speaking those aims that are characterizations of states of affairs in the world, rather than characterizations of internal states, and that are ends in themselves rather than means to further ends. Of course, we do value some things because they serve further ends—we may value an education because it offers us a chance to go to medical school. And we may want to go to medical school for yet further reasons. But this chain of reasons must stop somewhere. There must be some terminal values for which we can offer no justification. And it is these values, the ones that ground the others, that we wish to consider here.

At first blush it would seem that our ultimate concerns have the same status for us that chess playing has for Sargon: they are things toward which we strive, but for which we can offer no further justification, and which we may in some sense only dimly understand. How are they different, or is winning a chess game a value for Sargon as liberty, equality, and fraternity are for us?

In part they're different because interfering with a person's values might cause suffering, and Sargon doesn't suffer when we turn it off. But suppose that we could alter a person's values without making her suffer too—by brainwashing, hypnosis, Valium, and so on. Is doing so, therefore, proper? We think not. We think not because people care about the things they really value and that this caring has a weight separate from the suffering.

To see the caring independent of the suffering, consider this example. Imagine that a mother saw her child about to be run over by a car. Imagine that you offered her two choices: (1) she could save her child at the cost of great suffering to herself, or (2) she could take a drug that would make her forget that she ever had a child, and would make her become indifferent to the fact that this "stranger" was about to be run over. If she were to choose the second, we suggest, she could hardly be said to value her child. Rather, she values her own suffering. (Or at least she values her child little compared to her suffering.) She has emotions, of course, but no values. But if she takes the first, she demonstrates that she values her child *independent of any suffering or pain that the child's death might cause her.* And it is the fact that she would not make the second choice that gives rise to our understanding that to tamper with her *desire* to save her child is to do violence to her. Her willingness to make the second choice would show that her concern for her child has a different status from that of her suffering (the spectacle *of her choice* may provoke our pity, but we would have little reason to feel sympathy for her had she avoided the suffering).[10]

To have values, then, is not just to have ultimate purposes, or even to suffer at the sight of their being trampled, but to be unwilling to surrender that suffering at their expense. Only if she treats her concern about the life of her child as something beyond her will can this mother be said to value that child's life in a way that makes us loathe to tamper with her caring, or the object of her caring.

So Sargon, the chess-playing software, has some ultimate goal toward which it strives, which it doesn't understand and it doesn't value. Sargon doesn't suffer when we change its program, but even if we designed it to suffer, that wouldn't be enough to show that it valued chess as a terminal value. To show that, we would have to show that if we could offer it a different goal in a way that avoided the suffering, it would still not change. And if that were true of it, we should sympathize with it, and that should be enough to inhibit our changing its program.

Thus it isn't in principle that computers can't have values; it's just that we are sure our PC happens not to. And it is, presumably, because Chester, our retriever, doesn't value even his own life in this strong sense that we might offer him, or a dog just like him that we don't know personally, for legitimate medical research, so long as his pain and suffering were eliminated. In dealing with

Chester we want to protect what Chester himself cares about—his pains—but we feel it proper to expropriate to our own uses that which he doesn't care about, even, in the right context, his life. Sometimes people cease to care about their lives because, say, they are in intractable pain; they are willing to give up their lives to be spared the suffering. Our sympathy here is with their pain and we don't see their surrendering their valuing of their life as a betrayal.

Values, then, represent goals that a person has, that he cares about in an ultimate sense. They are ultimate in the sense that there can be no reasons offered to give them up or to take them on. Ultimate aims show the captivity of the will in a double sense, one which Sargon as well shows—the will must start from *some* premise, and another which Sargon doesn't show—that insofar as we were able to conceive of starting from a different premise we wouldn't. To value something is not simply to hold on to it as we would a particular geometry, as a starting point of calculation, but to hold on to it as something we would not, even could not, give up. This is not to say, of course, that people's values can't and don't change. It is just to say that for them to be values at the moment of having them they must be treated by the actor as things that they would not change. Because people with values really care about them we feel loathe to interfere with them.

Hector and His Values

One might ask: Does Hector really have any values in this strong sense? Do any of us? Perhaps not. But we believe humans capable of caring in this deep way; there may not be many mothers like the one above, mothers who pass Solomon's test, but the story nonetheless captures what it would be to value something utterly. Hector, whether or not he displays anything like a value in this strong sense, is still entitled to our protection and concern, just by virtue of his being human. And so too with Martians or more sophisticated computers. If we find that Martians are the kind of thing that has values, or that Compaqs are, then they too—all of them—deserve our sympathy.

Conclusion

We have tried to show that our conception of what it is to experience pain and emotion and what it is to value something all involve caring about something. Moreover, they all involve caring in a way that is beyond the will, beyond rational calculation of interest. A paramecium is, probably, too simple an organism for us to care much about. It is too simple to have much of a will, and things without wills are beneath our sympathy. But, we have tried to show, our sympathy for each other is also grounded in the limits of our will; creatures like my PC are too free for us to feel for.

Notes

1. Why do we call sympathy "moral"? By this we mean that it is wrong, all other things being equal, to do something to someone that arouses sympathy for that person (or animal). Further, the cases we shall analyze are clearly those with which the traditional study of morality has been concerned—for instance, why it is legitimate to dice plants but not people.

2. Miedaner (1981) has cleverly portrayed a rather basic machine that has marvelous tear-jerking properties—red lubricating oil, a "cry" like a beast in pain emitted on impact, etc. The machine is difficult to destroy; people's emotions get in the way. It elicits sympathy, perhaps, but this is because of its creator's giving it a mammal-like camouflage.

3. We thank Peter Badgio for making this distinction and the limitation of the argument clear to us.

4. We are endorsing the view, though not arguing for it, that all relations one bears to objects that are beyond one's will are morally

relevant in the sense of engaging our sympathy, that in deciding whether we owe someone sympathy a necessary question to raise is whether his plight is beyond or within his will.

5. One further point: We attempt to show the centrality of the notions of caring and the will in our treatment of others by showing their centrality to pain, emotions, and values. And we believe that these are the crucial psychological states in terms of justifying our feeling that we ought to leave something alone, but perhaps they aren't. Perhaps there are other equally, or more, important experiences that we haven't mentioned, experiences that don't involve caring or the will. Perhaps. But we can't think of any. We propose that it is just these aspects of human experience, the ones beyond calculation, beyond the will, that relate to our sympathy for each other and for other creatures toward whom we might have sympathy.

6. Laughing gas provides, perhaps, the most punctuate example of cases in which the sensory component of pain is isolated from concern about it, but more dramatic examples abound in the psychological literature. Beecher's (1959) observation that some soldiers suffering tremendous injuries reacted in an unusual way, sometimes even with euphoria, is the most dramatic finding. Because at the front line a serious injury meant release from combat, the injury produced entirely different reactions from those one would expect from the sensations considered alone, outside of the context of the soldiers lives. Lobotomy and leucotomy, too, are able to dissociate sensation from caring. Melzack, 1973, provides a useful summary of these clinical findings.

7. Not only is it difficult to act in the face of pain, it is difficult to control one's own thinking in its grip. Pain is *distracting*; while in pain it is hard to concentrate, follow an argument, pursue a flirtation. To be distracted has to do with finding it difficult to pay attention to what one wants to pay attention to. (Here we are using "wants" in the sense of a final decision, in the sense of what one wills.) So, to speak of distraction is to speak of desire, the will. To know that someone is distracted is to know something about what she desires. To speak of a distracted Martian requires us to be intimate with at least some of her wants.

8. Physicians sometimes decide that patients are "making a big deal out of a little pain," the force of the claim being that the patient

wouldn't experience pain to such a degree if "he didn't really want to." Holding aside the epistemological issue of how a physician could know, we point out that once she believes that the patient could choose to care less, she treats the patient differently, less sympathetically.

9. Block (1981) has an ingenious argument showing that something that could pass a Turing test is still not intelligent. And, it would seem, the concepts of intelligence and purposiveness are linked. Thus, there might be some ways, or even a way, for Sargon to beat me without really having any purpose at all. But still the form of "psychologism" that Block argues for simply shows that there are some limits on the ways that a thing can do what it does and still be counted as intelligent. The argument does not show that the way Sargon does it fails to display intelligence, or purposiveness. Since Sargon calculates, in fact, Block's way of cheating is ruled out.

10. A skeptic could argue that even *choosing* the first option (not to suffer) would cause so much guilt that the mother, for strictly hedonistic reasons, would not do so. This may be interpreted in two ways. First, the mother might be ashamed in front of Mephistopheles, or another audience, to show herself to be *that* sort of person. If this is the case, we can arrange for her to choose in complete privacy or, if she prefers, before an approving group. Or second, the argument might be that, even alone, the idea of *being* the sort of person who chooses the first option is just too painful. While this conception is close to some conceptions of moral acting, to be absolutely sure her motives are proper, we can offer her an additional drug to ensure that she will not mind being *that* sort of person too, or a drug that will guarantee that she, and everyone else, will be deluded into believing she is a heroine. In less fanciful sorts of trials, pretexts are often used in place of drugs.

References

Beecher, H. K. (1959). *Measurement of subjective responses.* London: Oxford University Press, 1959.

Block, N. (1981). Psychologism and behaviorism. *The Philosophical Review, 90,* 5–43.

Dennett, D. C. (1978). Why you can't make a computer that feels pain. In *Brainstorms* (pps. 190–229). Cambridge, MA.: Bradford Books.

Miedaner, T. (1981). The soul of Martha, a beast. In D. Hofstadter & D. Dennett (Eds.), *The mind's I: Fantasies and reflections on self and soul* (pp. 100–106). New York: Basic Books.

Melzack, R. (1973). *The puzzle of pain.* New York: Basic Books.

Rey, G. (1980). Functionalism and the emotions. In A. Rorty, *Explaining emotions* (pp. 163–197). Berkeley: University of California Press.

Silver, M. (1985). "Purposive behavior" in psychology and philosophy: A history. In M. Frese and J. Sabini (Eds.), *Goal directed behavior: The concept of action in psychology* (pps. 3–19). Hillsdale, N.J.: Erlbaum.

Taylor, C. (1982). Consciousness. In P. Secord (Ed.), *Explaining human behavior* (pp. 35–53). Beverly Hills, Calif.: Sage.

4

Sincerity

Feelings and Constructions in Making a Self

Once a student complimented one of us on a lecture, pointing out several of its virtues, but at the same time mentioning further insights we might have provided but didn't quite, and also how the lecture fit so well with his career interests. A dramaturgic, social constructivist perspective might offer this analysis: the dear undergraduate had made use of social conventions in presenting himself as an attentive, committed, discerning example of the student type. He had constructed a self out of these objective, shared materials. But, by laying it on too thick, he had not only failed to present himself as an attentive student but instead wound up looking like a toady. Still, questions remain: Was the compliment in fact sincere? Did it represent his real self? Was he an inept con man or an inept but attentive, committed, discerning student?

Social constructivism and dramaturgy (cf. Berger & Luckmann, 1966; Goffman, 1959) do not respond well to questions of sincerity, and hence seem to ignore the real self. (Messinger was, perhaps, the first to raise this point against Goffman's analysis of the social life; Messinger, Sampson, & Towne, 1962.) Ignoring "authentic feelings" is an affront to common sense. People get worked up about authenticity, genuineness, sincerity. We shall analyze these commonsense notions and articulate them with the social-constructivist approach to capture our sense of a real person, and find a place for authentic feelings and action.[1]

In *Ulysses,* Stephen Dedalus raises the issue of sincerity poignantly: "You wouldn't kneel down to pray for your mother on her deathbed when she asked you. Why? Because you have the cursed Jesuit strain in you, only it's injected in the wrong way" (Joyce, 1934/1961, p. 8). Stephen loved his mother, wanted to comfort her, yet could not without violating a principle: he was no longer a believer and, thus, praying would be insincere, a betrayal.

But of what could his betrayal be? Were he still a believer he could betray his God, but having given up God he gave up anything he could betray—anything except his self. Some scholars tell us (cf. Lyons, 1978; Trilling, 1972) that the self is an increasingly, perhaps newly, valued object of our moral and aesthetic concern.[2]

According to Trilling (1972), sincerity is a match between avowal and feeling. Our questions become, then: How do feelings bear on the real self (in the various senses of the term feeling)? And how are feelings related to the social constructivist model?

We begin with the kinds of feeling that are immediate, compelling, genuine, those feelings that we cannot doubt, though we can dissimulate—that is, pains, itches, impulses—feelings as *episodes* (they occupy consciousness over a temporal stretch, cf. Ryle, 1949). We shall then work our way out to feelings that are not episodic; we start with these because we suspect that they are prototypes of the commonsense notion of the genuine.

Pain

Pain is surely the most compelling feeling; it can occupy our minds with an immediacy and exclusivity that no other feeling or thought can. Despite this, pain reports are typically not assessed by the concept of sincerity; we think of pain reports as true or false, not sincere or insincere. Still pain does have a role, though an indirect one, in our thinking about the real self, and for that reason the dramaturgic or social constructivist position must give it a place in our self-knowledge. Consider an example of pain, and its role in self-knowledge.

A friend has a touch of arthritis, but he has offered to help us move—out of friendship and because he, too, is moving next month. He is, however, known for his laziness as well as his good intentions. On the day we move he continuously mentions his twinges of pain—real twinges. Eventually we give him a beer and suggest he sit the move out.

His pain reports figure in our assessment of his sincerity and our understanding of his real self. Specifically, his griping leads us to doubt the sincerity of his offer, or at least his current willingness to help. And we can believe this though we believe there is, in Trilling's words, a congruence between avowal and feeling—each arthritic twinge is avowed. His sincerity, on the other hand, would be less in question had he gamely pretended not to feel the pain he indubitably did feel. Making consciousness transparent to others, then, is hardly an adequate account of how to act sincerely. Reports of states of consciousness affect our assessment of self, not just by their veracity but also through (a) the "meaning," objective force within a socially constructed normative order, of those avowals; and (b) the relation between what one is doing with those avowals and the obligations, values, and commitments to which the making of the avowals relate. In particular, our friend knew, or ought to have known, what offer, in this context, his complaint would provoke, and he knew, or ought to have known, the relation of the offer to sit out the move to his commitments and obligations. So while in this story about immediate feelings pain does play a role, so too do conventions. And the interesting work done by the pain in the construction of the self is as much a product of that social context as it is of the pain qua experience. There is, however, another role for pain in the construction of the self.

Imagine that our friend could not have stifled or ignored his pain, that he really could not have carried the furniture. He wanted to display and have a helpful self; his pain obstructed his desire. Pain, here, is a constraint on the will and on the selves we would be.

Pain, then, figures in the selves we can create in two ways: in the first example, it was an element in a construction completed by convention, and in the second, it figures as a limit on possible selves.

IMPULSES

Itches fill consciousness too, and in addition they naturally impel action—scratching. Impulses, too, can be felt; like itches (and pains), they are episodic and are connected to action or the desire to act. And in a proper context the question of sincerity does depend on their presence.

Imagine a young salesperson, Sue, with her avuncular, well-meaning, but quite stuffy sales manager, Bill. They are finalizing, for the 100th time, plans for the next show. Prudence, politeness, and even affection dictate an expression of interest, reflection, and most of all, appreciation. Although she responds with delight to his retread wit, she also finds herself struggling with, and even succumbing to, disrespectful fantasies, daydreams, and other discreditable impulses.[3] Is her presentation sincere?

To be sure, her enthusiasm is feigned, but is the affection expressed in the enthusiasm phony? Considered as expressions of interest in the details of the plan, her actions are insincere, but considered as expressions of affection they might be sincere. Still, her acts *avow* interest (affection, though expressed, is not avowed), which gives that expression a special status in judging the sincerity of her *acts*. But the sincerity of her *self*, deriving from the sincerity of her acts, also turns on what she was trying to do.

If she was feigning in order to avoid hurt feelings, then her feigning expressed kindness; the kindness, at least, is sincere. Thus, we cannot decide whether she is sincere just by first deciding whether her acts are sincere, in the sense of expressing impulses, and then summing. Thus the relation between the transparency of action and sincerity is complex, depending, in part, on intent.

Impulses and Values

Sometimes students come by to discuss grades. On occasion one will become so upset that she will cry. Now this is distressing—distressing to us, though, to be sure, more distressing to her. Tears give rise to impulse, the impulse to comfort. But the idea of a professor involves grading fairly. This idea competes with the impulse. What is the sincere thing to do, which is the real me? On the one hand, there is a directly felt impulse; on the other, a conception of oneself connected to roles and institutions that one values. The impulse is more immediate. But, if one actually values the institution, role, and idea, to comfort is to betray, not express, the real self. But, it might be argued, why not comfort, too; why not do both?

One answer is that the expression of the comforting impulse cannot be sincere; in *this* context it cannot be. To comfort, in the way the students want comforting, is to undermine the vantage from which the comforting can be offered: she needs comfort from her teacher, not from her friends; she needs to be told, not that she is a fine person generally but that her teacher has found her to be a good student. And that comfort cannot be offered, or at least it cannot be sincerely offered, even though the impulse is genuinely felt. There is another reason it cannot be sincerely expressed.

Sincere expressions of feeling are understood to be connected to action that matters. The relation between them is not, or not only, that the feelings goad the acts but that the acts express the feelings. A sincere expression of the comfort one might dearly wish to offer would have to be matched by a corresponding action: a grade change. Sincere words uncoupled from consequential acts fail to engage the world and the self.

Even so, the unexpressed impulse to comfort does play a role in the self. I might have told her, "Sorry, but you do not deserve a grade change," without the slightest urge to comfort. And there is an important difference between these two cases: resisting the impulse shows that my resisting a grade change is not from indifference, but principle—that I am not a cold fish, but a responsible professor.

Values, roles, and institutions upheld against impulses, then, may reveal the self. It is also true that succumbing to impulses would reveal a self, too—one that succumbs to impulses and does not live up to values.

There are some impulses that reveal a self just by their presence. A scoutmaster who feels sexual impulses toward his charges may recoil in horror at the self this shows him to have, even though he never has, and believes he never will, act on them.[4] But interesting questions about the self, unlike this example, are rarely questions about what urges a person has, for the reason Freud noticed—for the most part we have the same urges.

Emotion

If there is a place where the notion that being sincere is a matter of fitting avowal to experience and that the self is revealed through that experience, it seems to be with the emotions. But consider: One night after dinner, while you are stretched out before the fire, your lover turns to you and asks, "Do you love me?" Regrettably, despite the fire and the mood, your consciousness is dominated by a gas pain. How should you answer? What would be the sincere thing to say, the thing that would express your self? "No," because at the moment you have a gas pain? Surely not.

Our emotion terms, including love, have a dual use (cf. Ryle, 1949; Kenny, 1963); in one use they refer to episodes, in another they refer to dispositions—dispositions not only to have episodes but to act in certain ways. In particular, announcements of love involve more than true reports of current states. A true description of current states of affection or passion is a mockery if the speaker intends to abscond with the silverware the next day. Commitments to the future, of course, must be assessed in relation to the other commitments a person has made; commitments that conflict are deceptive, even self-deceptive. But aspects of the self other than competing commitments can also vitiate commitments—for example, one's capacities, temperament, and so on, can make particular commitments impossible to fulfill. Thus the coherence of a person's commitments and their relation to broader aspects of the self are relevant to an assessment of the sincerity of the announcement of an emotional state. Thus your lover's question and your answer announce, not that at the moment you are filled with passion, affection, or concern, but that you do experience such episodes and that you are inclined to act in the ways that people who love each other act. In this way the question asks about previous episodes, predictions of future episodes, and commitments to behavior. Moreover, it is clear that your self is revealed in this broader, dispositional sense of emotion, rather than in the narrower sense that overlaps with impulse. Let us consider an example of another emotion, one that seems more closely connected to episodes of consciousness: anger.

Imagine that someone has done something to you that has caused you pain, and imagine that he asks you, "Are you angry with me?" Let us consider the various states you might be in, and the sincere response that follows from each of them.

You might at the moment be occupied by the pain you are feeling rather than by the offensiveness of his behavior. In this sense, you are not now *feeling* angry. But it would obviously be misleading for you simply to reply no. Although this does express your current state, it misleads about the way your relationship has been affected by his act. In that way, it misleads about who you are. Now let us consider the reverse case. Suppose you believe that you are at the moment filled with impulses to seek revenge, but you know just as clearly that on reflection you will decide that it really was not his fault, or that it was, but it was not much of a fault. Here a simple yes would be just as misleading as the simple no would have been in the previous case. Further, for you to express your rage in a temper tantrum would reveal little about your self except your immaturity (cf. Sabini & Silver, 1982). Now let us focus on an important role episodes do play in emotion, sincerity, and the self.

Emotions are, after all, not just a matter of judgment. There is a certain poignancy in the plight of someone asked about his love who wants to answer yes because he cares about, respects, and recognizes the virtues of (even romantic virtues of) his interrogator, but not only does not at this moment feel anything but who suspects he will not in the future. He may answer yes, perhaps in the hope things will change, but his yes is hollow and he feels it. So, in good faith, this lover may wish to commit himself to what love implies, and yet, without the experience—the episode—his avowal is hollow, insincere. The further complications of experienced feelings—hollowness, spontaneity, and integrity—we must leave for another place.

Questions about emotional states, then, may require reports or predictions of episodes, perhaps even episodes of consciousness. But their sincere report involves more than that; it involves, for example, commitments. The pragmatic force of reports of emotional states do, in most contexts, require us to consider the relation between these immediate experiences we are having and the more stable selves we know, or wish, ourselves to have.

Feelings, the Self, and the Will

All the senses of feeling we have considered so far are, and are seen as, outside of the will—we have pains, impulses, and emotions whether we welcome them or not. (See chapter 3 on the relations of pain, emotion, and values to the will.) We may decide to stifle them, but they must be there to stifle. In this sense, they are independent of our beliefs about what is appropriate, in our best interest, fashionable, and so on. They show us the natures we have, whether to move us to transcend them or to celebrate them, even though the sincerity of their expression is constructed by their relations with convention and context.

Without contrasting a civilized veneer with a genuine nature, we can see that these tugs are important reminders, and even obstacles to self-deception. Sexual arousal in response to our neighbor's wife does not mean that our self is tainted, but it does mean that we cannot have the comfortable belief that it will not be tainted because of an absence of temptation.

Feelings as Beliefs: Intuitions

There is a nonepisodic notion of feeling, feeling as belief. Sometimes feeling means belief (as in I feel Nicaragua will be invaded), and sincerity in this sense has to do with beliefs' matching expression. In this sense of feeling the sincere person does not have to feel anything like an itch; many of our beliefs are implicit—we do not constantly say to ourselves that the world is round though we believe it, even when we are not thinking it. But we do not call all beliefs feelings. Which beliefs are?

Admission committees decide whether students should be admitted to departments. It is common enough to report that one just does not feel that an applicant is right for the program. But this would be a foolish comment if the applicant expressed an interest in relativity theory (the file mistakenly wound up in the psychology department). But the comment would also be foolish if the speaker had not opened the folder. We use "feeling" when we are claiming tacit knowledge, a belief grounded in aspects of the case that we cannot articulate; such claims are assertions of belief hedged by the actor's inability to point to evidence for them. In such cases, we talk of feelings, intuitions, impressions, hunches, and so forth. (Impressions of personality, because of the inherent uncertainty and difficulty we have in saying just what they are based on, or for that matter should be based on, are particularly likely to be called feelings—"I don't know, I just feel that she isn't trustworthy.") We do not use feeling to announce patent or obviously ascertainable facts. Distortions of known facts are lies; distortions of feelings are insincere. The following example will clarify this point.

Imagine a surgeon asked by a patient, "Doctor, is it cancer?" Assuming a competent pathologist, and a routine tumor, this is a matter which has a fact, and is a question about that fact, not feelings. But suppose after the grim news is announced the patient presses, "What are my chances?" And the surgeon replies, "I feel you really have a good chance." Here, presumably, the surgeon is being asked about, and reporting (sincerity or not), her clinical *judgment,* her *intuitions*. Here sincerity is an issue because the facts do not, or do not quite, determine the prognosis. Were the patient to inquire about the doctor's sincerity, he would be asking her whether she is expressing her real impression in light of the facts of his case and her accumulated years of clinical wisdom. One sense of sincerity, then, has to do with expressing beliefs of a certain sort, in correspondence with what the person actually believes.

We have argued, then, that an actor's sincerity in expressing a judgment is in question only when (a) she cannot articulate the grounds of the judgment *and* the judgment is uncertain (actors have no grounds for believing that 2 + 2 = 4, though they are certain,[5] and this is not an issue of sincerity); and when (b) that judgment *is* based on evidence to some degree (announcements about the worth of students while obviously not having seen their records are equally disqualified). This reading of sincerity has implications for understanding those facets of self related to intuition, understanding, even wisdom.

Why should judgments under uncertainty be important in creating selves? For one thing, in such circumstances the sum of an individual's experiences, reflections, habits, values, and so on is brought to bear on the problem—wisdom replaces algorithm.[6]

This has an ironic, though by now anticipated, implication. Whether a particular judgment is or is not an expression of the self depends on cultural and historical facts, on what is socially shared, what has been socially constructed. As tests replace "clinical judgment," room for the kinds of judgments that express the self shrinks. The replacement of the enormous store of intuition that neurologists once treasured by the mechanics of CAT scanning is a current example of just such a development. Technique is, no doubt, more reliable, but less engaging: flying by the seat of one's pants may be more dangerous than computer-guided approaches, but it is the sort of thing from which stories can be told, heroes made, selves constructed.

Romanticism, with its concentration on the centrality of intuition, also involves an affirmation of selves. It values people for their accumulated experience, their wisdom. Formal system, romanticism's foil, replaces wisdom with technique and hence squeezes the person out of the world. Weber, the rationalist, saw all of this and noticed the disenchantment of the world that technique produces.

We have argued here that the knowing self, then, is expressed in judgments having a particular relation to their evidence; they are feelings—judgments, intuitions—that reflect the evidence in combination with reflection on the actor's own, personal, subjective (if you like) experience. This experience is always socially located, a particular biography created from the materials of a shared biography (Berger & Luckmann, 1966).

We have seen that episodic feelings are informative about the self in relation to a person's goals and desires. We are now in a better position to understand how desires, and so on, relate to the self.

A Summary of the Dramaturgic Model, Sincerity, and Feelings

The dramaturgic perspective is incomplete. Feelings do play a role in the construction of the self, in part because episodic feelings are at the limit of the will—our friend would have helped us move but cannot because of his pain, and the lover who wishes he felt what he does not are bumping up against these limits. Further feelings as hunches and desires sum up a unique history and display commitments. When we started it appeared as if enacted roles and genuine feelings were necessarily in opposition. Since sincerity was a matter of feeling, of conscious contents, of impulses and tugs, any model that dealt with rules, standards, manipulated impressions—social constructions—could not approach sincerity. We have argued instead that sincerity, even sincerity seen as a match between feelings and avowals, requires rules, standards, and even manipulations—the constructed stuff. This objective context enabled feelings to play the various roles we have identified in the question of sincerity. The objective standards and the experienced episodes are intimately linked and not in opposition.

A Postscript on the Self

We have considered, then, relations among feelings, in the various senses of that term, and being sincere. And we have seen some of the ways that sincere expressions reveal the self. But there is one important issue about sincerity that we have not yet taken up—the fact that Dedalus saw being sincere as something of value in itself. Some have argued (Lyons, 1978) that Dedalus's position, his refusal to kneel and pray before his dying mother because to do so would be insincere, would be unintelligible to the Middle Ages, odd to the Renaissance, and only at home with Boswell, Rousseau, and those who came later. We will not argue here about why this change has come about, but it is important to see that sincerity is not a timeless value. Consider how Rousseau starts his *Confession* (1781/1954):

> I have resolved on an enterprise which has no precedent, and which, once complete, will have no imitator. My purpose is to display to my kind a portrait in every way true to nature, and the man I shall portray will be myself.
> Simply myself. I know my own heart and understand my fellow man. But I am made unlike anyone I have ever met; I will even venture to say that I am like no one in the whole world. I may be no better, but at least I am different.

The prevalent antihero in current literature perhaps attests to an even greater emphasis on authenticity, the genuine display of self in spite of the warts. The antihero is one with traditional vices, but with the saving "virtues" of integrity, honesty, and sincerity. Mersault, in *The Stranger* (Camus, 1942), on the day of his mother's death refuses to mourn—a step beyond Stephen—goes to the beach, starts an affair, advises a pimp on how to punish his whore, and, more or less by happenstance, kills someone. Yet Mersault is sincere. He not only understands and accepts what he feels and does but also is willing to face being condemned to a death sentence rather than to posture to pretend that his feelings and perceptions were other than, "nicer" than, they were. Mersault is executed because of his sincerity, not because of his killing a man. The reader sees, or at least is intended to see, Mersault despite his rather nasty flaws as something of a hero. Mersault completes Rousseau's project. If showing oneself warts and all is acceptable to Rousseau, it is the only test of worth for Mersault. Finally, sincerity is not *a* virtue; it is for this extreme antihero the only virtue.

Would Chaucer or Cervantes or Montaigne or Dante have found anything of value in him? Would they have found our seeing him as a hero, or even an antihero, sensible? That we can but they could not suggests how current our concern, not with our selves—selfishness may be a historical constant—but with our self is.

Notes

We dedicate this chapter to the memory of Stanley Milgram, our mentor.

1. Our method shall be conceptual. That is, we shall describe a range of examples in terms that do not involve sincerity. We then ask how, having given the examples as we have described them, we have to (given our concepts) describe them in terms of sincerity. The payoff is an understanding of the concept of sincerity in relation to the concepts that have entered into our original descriptions. Of course the virtues of the piece depend on our starting points—as it does for any scientific work. For more on this see Sabini and Silver (1982, chap. 1).

2. The romantic view of the self requires coherence not only on moral but on aesthetic grounds—one's experience, values, life should in some sense fit.

3. Sometimes instead of an impulse we are frustrated by an in-

ability to concentrate. But this surely would play the same role in the story.

4. Sometimes impulses can help us discover aspects of ourselves. For instance, a homosexual may have originally felt restless in heterosexual roles without knowing why. This restlessness, in combination with various sexual impulses toward members of the same sex, may lead to a realization or discovery of the self as a homosexual, one confirmed by the feeling of *relief* experienced when she identified herself to herself, a gay community, and perhaps the straight world as homosexual (Warren & Ponse, 1977).

5. Ironically, the two front-running candidates for indubitability—mathematical truths and sensations—have only a tangential relevance to the self, or to sincerity.

6. Still, given a choice between wise selves and well-constructed algorithms, the actor with high pragmatic stakes might do well to put aside sincerity for certainty. (Cf. Gould, 1983, for a discussion of the tradeoff.)

References

Berger, P., & Luckmann, T. (1966). *The social construction of reality.* New York: Doubleday.

Camus, A. (1942). *The stranger.* J. O'Brien (Trans.). New York: Vintage.

Goffman, E. (1959). *The presentation of self in everyday life.* New York: Doubleday.

Gould, S. J. (1983, July 21). Review of L. Thomas *The youngest science. New York Review of Books, 30,* 12–14.

Joyce, J. (1934/1961). *Ulysses.* New York: Vintage.

Kenny, A. (1963). *Action, emotion and will.* New York: Humanities Press.

Lyons, J. (1978). *The invention of the self.* Carbondale, Ill.: Southern Illinois University Press.

Messinger, S. E., Sampson, H., & Towne, R. D. (1962). Life as theater: Some notes on the dramaturgic approach to social reality. *Sociometry, 25,* 98–110.

Rousseau, J. (1781/1954). *The confessions.* J. M. Cohen (Trans.). Baltimore: Penguin.

Ryle, G. (1949). *The concept of mind.* New York: Barnes & Noble.

Sabini, J., & Silver, M. (1982). *Moralities of everyday life.* New York: Oxford University Press.

Trilling, L. (1972). *Sincerity and authenticity.* Cambridge, Mass.: Harvard University Press.

Warren, C., & Ponse, B. (1977). The existential self in the gay world. In J. Douglas & J. Johnson (Eds.), *Existential sociology.* New York: Cambridge University Press.

5

Loyalty as Good and Duty

A Critique of Stocker

Friendship, community, fellow feeling, and love are all parts of a good life, a virtuous life. They also anchor several recent criticisms of moral theory. According to some critics, one cannot be a good Kantian or consequentialist while being a good friend. These traditions neglect essential features of the good life for two reasons. First, at least for Kant, proper feelings, desires, and impulses are unwilled and, hence, not moral. Elsewhere (see chapter 2), we argue that there are elements of the good life that are not moral. Second, morality appears to require objectivity—rights, duties, and rational choice should be applicable to anyone who embodies abstract features. This impersonality seems to preclude genuine love for a particular, concrete individual. Stocker (1976) develops this attack on Kantianism and consequentialism in detail. We think, however, that with some alteration we can defend these traditions against his attack.

As Stocker sees it, the call to duty (or for that matter, utility or the good) is too impersonal to support relationships. To be in love with someone or to be someone's friend involves desires, sentiments, and attitudes toward that person, but to be a moral agent involves desires, sentiments, and attitudes toward duty or the good. Stocker claims that the conflict between duty and friendship is so extreme as to produce a 'moral schizophrenia': someone who tries to be both moral and a friend cannot, logically, bring his motives in line with his reasons. This disharmony he sees as a poverty of spirit that philosophy should cure, not create.

Our aim in this chapter is to show that this poverty of spirit, this disharmony, is not iatrogenic but environmental. Circumstances may conspire to force on a moral person a life, or a moment, that is cold, austere, and alienated; we don't believe it is the moral theories Stocker criticizes that prevent us from living a good life. On the other hand, we believe that Stocker is right in his intuition that these theories fail to justify much that is central to a good life.

STOCKER ON GENUINE LOVE

Stocker asks us to consider love. He argues, "First, if you try to carry on a relationship for the sake of goodness, there is no essential commitment even to that activity, much less to the persons involved. So far as goodness is involved, you might as well love as ski, or write poetry, or eat a nice meal or . . ." (Stocker, 1976, p. 458). His argument is that to love someone is to commit oneself to that person, but to act so as to maximize the good is to commit oneself to something else—the good. Genuine love must be for the sake of the other, but a utilitarian can't love because a utilitarian must act for the sake of the good. "Do you love me or my goodness, the good you get from loving me?," Stocker might ask.

Stocker goes on to argue that the reason for this paradox is that

> What is lacking in these theories is simply—or not so simply—the person. For love, friendship, affection, fellow-feeling, and community all require that the other person be an essential part of what is valued. The person—not merely the person's general values nor even the person-qua-producer-or-possessor-of-general-values—must be valued. The defect of these theories in regard to love, to take one case, is not that they do not value love (which, often, they do not) but that they do not value the beloved. (Stocker, 1976, p. 459)

This certainly seems like a problem, but we shall make a different diagnosis.

Motives for Loving, Ulterior and Intrinsic

We suggest that Stocker sees a paradox here because he is criticizing a particular kind of utilitarianism: Moore's, one that sees the good in loving to be detachable from the loving. But the good of love, or at least one aspect of love, cannot be detached from the loving. Suppose that one sees the 'goodness' of loving as Ryle (1949) sees the pleasure in doing crossword puzzles, as in the activity itself. Is the schizophrenia that Stocker points to present in this analysis?

If what makes an act of love or friendship good is that it was done for another's sake, then explaining it by saying that it was done for another's sake does not compete with an explanation that says it was done because it was good. There is no risk of schizophrenia from acting for the good and for another's sake if what makes an act good is that it is for another's sake. Stocker asks his utilitarian lover: "Did you do it for my sake or because it was good?" This has the form of a question about ulterior motives—

did you do it for my sake or for money? But when the good gained is not (conceptually) detachable from the doing, the good can't be an ulterior motive. Stocker's criticism assumes that an actor cannot be characterized in two ways at once. But consider a parallel case to see that we can, at least sometimes, be characterized as acting for two things at once.

Suppose a musician were asked why she practiced the clarinet—for the sake of having a good tone or for the sake of the beautiful? Must she be schizophrenic to answer: "Both, indeed it is by practicing for the sake of the tone of my clarinet that I am practicing for the sake of the beautiful"? The reason she is not schizophrenic is that music is one embodiment of the beautiful. Of course, a beautiful tone could detract from the beauty of a performance, and in such a case a person is acting for the sake of the beauty of her tone, sacrificing the beauty of the piece. But, on Stocker's analysis of love, loving is necessarily a good and acting for the sake of another is necessarily loving. Loving is one embodiment of the good.

One can have the view that some goods are not detachable from activities and still be a utilitarian in the sense of urging utilitarian procedures for deciding what to do; for instance, one can still enjoin people to weigh their good and the good for others in deciding what to do. The problem Stocker has with Moore is not with the utilitarian part of his ethical theory but with Moore's particular account of the good. All of this is not to argue that utilitarianism is an adequate ethical view, nor is it to argue that all goods are activities rather than the consequences of activities.

Loving Someone in Particular

So far we have dealt with Stocker's objection that utilitarianism sees loving someone as a means to a further end: obtaining the good. But he has a second objection: that a utilitarian cannot love someone *in particular*. To see the difference between these two objections, notice that the question, "Do you love me?" has at least two readings; one places the emphasis on the "love" the other on the "me." The first reading, which we have already discussed, asks whether one truly loves (as opposed to acting out of some other motive). The second reading asks whether it is *me* you love (as opposed to someone, or something, else). The peculiarity of this question can be seen by examining a related one: "Do you love me for my mind?" As anyone who has been asked this question knows, you can't win, no matter how you answer. And this is what Stocker calls attention to. If you say yes, then you would love anyone with the same mind, and thus your beloved is merely an embodiment of a feature. This doesn't, however, attack the *purity* of your motives, the sincerity of your love. In such a case you truly love; what is at issue is whether you love this particular person or just that sort of mind. But if you answer no, then you love for no reason, making love necessarily irrational. And that it is sometimes irrational none of us doubts; what we might like to resist is the view that it is necessarily irrational. (Needless to say, answering "No, I love you for your charming accent" does nothing to relieve the discomfort, because this just trades one feature for another. Nor does it help to list a collection of features; this makes it less likely that another will take your beloved's place, but it leaves loves still a matter of odds.)

The reason for this dilemma, as Stocker notes, is that *reasons* must implicate abstract features; they recommend equally any and all bearers of them. The trouble has to do with the interplay between love, which is of a particular, and reasons, which are abstract.

Love, Loyalty, and Shared History

What is needed to rescue love is something abstract enough to be a reason but specific to the person we happen to love. Shared history can do part of the job. Stocker asks us to reflect on someone who claims to be in love, but who continuously checks to see whether there isn't someone else who embodies more of what she finds good. This is not a portrait of love. We suggest it is not because such a lover gives no weight to the fact, accidental in prospect but necessary in retrospect, that she happens to have been involved with this particular person.

We argue, then, that features we find valuable are causally relevant to a relationship, and that features are detachable. But the loyalty that grows from shared history is a reason to love a particular person, is independent of these features, and is not a feature of the person. And this is also true of friendship, fellow feeling, and community; one reason we stick with our friends and community, a reason in addition to those we can offer to newcomers, is simply that they are and have been our friends and community.

A loyalty developed from your shared history is one reason to love someone, but there is another as well. Relationships involve "shared projects"—plans that reach into the future. Another reason to stick with the one you love is that to change loves is to abandon projects. And fitfulness is hardly the well-lived life.

Our argument, then, is that utilitarianism can find a good in human relationships that is independent of the detachable qualities of those involved, so long as it recognizes that there is a good in the loyalty that develops, and can only develop, in our experience of forming projects, and having formed projects, with particular people. Recognizing this, we can avoid the schizophrenia that Stocker finds inherent in loving people for reasons, while at the same time we can recognize that there is something beyond the qualities they embody that should lead us to love them.

This does not mean that we should stick with people no matter what; our argument does not require that having sustained relationships with the same people should outweigh every other good. Sincere love need not be unconditional. We simply propose that loyalty has value. How much value it has is a separate question from whether it is valuable.

Any theory of the good, if it is to fit our experience, has to give value to loving a person independent of anything one gets from that love. Any such theory will have to see loyalty and shared projects as important human goods, though not necessarily as the only human good, not as a good for which we should be willing to pay any price. Any theory of human evils will have to find a place for betrayal, an evil that robs our relationships to friends, lovers, or communities of loyalty and the possibility of shared projects.

Stocker on Kant

Stocker also argues that a consistent Kantian can't love. He offers us an example to consider. Imagine that you are recuperating from a long illness and someone you take to be a friend visits repeatedly, buoying your spirits. But suppose that your friend announces that he has merely come out of duty, that he saw himself as having a general duty to cheer the sick and you were the easiest opportunity for him to discharge this duty. Is this acting out of friendship? Stocker asks. Surely there is something hollow in this. But why?

The Duties of Friendship

There are two related issues here. First, imagine that by virtue of your illness you have become a tremendous bore; pain or concern about your recovery has effaced those qualities that spontaneously attract the attention of anyone open to the good. Then why would someone visit? Surely out of duty; what other reason could there be? But to decide whether he is really your friend we need to ask: from what does his duty follow? It might be that *he* has a duty to cheer you up just because he is your friend. Insofar as he acts out of a duty that is itself dependent on being a friend, then the conflict between friendship and duty is resolved. So there is no necessary conflict between duty and friendship. For Kantian theory too, loyalty (duties to particular people) bridges the gap between abstract moral demands and a concern with particular people.

But, some have argued, loyalty (of which visiting sick friends is one manifestation) cannot be a duty because it is not generalizable. Loyalty involves duties to someone not by virtue of some feature that person embodies, but because of the history of that person's relationship to us. And, it has been argued, a true duty must be dependent only on features that the object of our duty embodies. This argument against loyalty as a duty is parallel to an argument against loyalty as a good in utilitarianism; both arguments assume that moral decisions must be based on abstract features that must in every case be detachable from their particular embodiments. Both look to abstraction and detachability as marking the distinction between the objective and the subjective, reason and habit, the real and the chimerical. But must loyalty be sacrificed to the objectivity of morality?

We argue that it need not. There is an important sense in which the obligation of loyalty is generalizable; the person who argues that loyalty is a duty claims that loyalty is a duty for all who happen to be in a sustained relationship with others. This duty is objective, real, beyond the will, if you like. We can consistently will that everyone should be loyal to their friends, visit them in the hospital.

If we accept the notion that one has an obligation from loyalty to cheer up particular people, and this duty itself follows from friendship, then a person can act out of friendship and duty at once. Stocker's example in which our friend responds that he acted not out of friendship but out of a general duty to cheer people up certainly offends our intuitions about how a life should be lived, but we suggest that it offends them by failing to recognize particular duties to our friends. This is not a defect of duty-based moral conceptions per se, but of duty-based conceptions that fail to include our intuitions that we do have special duties to our friends by virtue of their being our friends. But there is another issue raised by Stocker's example, one that has to do, not with whether one acts out of duty to a particular person or out of a general duty, but with whether one acts out of duty at all.

To see this, let us imagine that as before because of your illness you become a bore, but perhaps also because of the illness you fail to notice it. Your friend, being considerate, gives every appearance, however, of responding with spontaneous interest to each of your stories of the rigors of hospital life. Now let us imagine that for some reason you ask your friend directly whether he visits you every day out of duty or a spontaneous desire to spend the afternoon with you. And he replies, "Out of duty"—not in this case out of duty to people in general but out of a particular duty to you as his friend. Again, there is a hollowness. But this time not because your friend is not really a friend. After all, if he thinks you are so boring, what other reason than friendship could he have for visiting so often; his persistence in the face of your tediousness is a tribute to the genuineness of his friendship.

The problem here is that your discovery of why your friend was so attentive humiliates you. And being humiliated, even unintentionally, by a friend is a very undesirable state of affairs. But what did your friend do to produce this lamentable state?

Surely it did not follow from his doing his duty to visit you; rather, it was a consequence of his making clear to you that he acted out of duty rather than pleasure. The culprit is truth-telling, not visiting. It is, perhaps, a special claim of Kantian morality that your duty to speak the truth overrides even your duty not to hurt a friend. But this is a defect, if it is a defect, of that special variant of duty-based ethics.

As Stocker sees, there is something painful and repulsive about doing things for your friends without finding the doing in the slightest attractive. But the repulsiveness does not come from recognizing and acting on duty. There is always the possibility of tragedy in human life; one kind of tragedy we know we might face is that those we love might, through fate, lose those qualities that attracted us to them in the first place. In establishing relationships we risk finding ourselves moved by duty to do things that give us no pleasure. But what should we say about someone who cares for his friend, even though his friend is no longer able to offer the very pleasures that provoked the friendship? What one misses in Stocker's analysis is some sense of how *lucky* one must be to have one's desires correspond to one's reasons. Even Aristotle, who, as much as any moralist, saw happiness in the proper formation of character, conceded a large role for good fortune in the ability to be happy.

Summary

We have argued, then, that both utilitarianism and Kantianism can accommodate love, friendship, fellow-feeling, and community. To do so, utilitarianism must count the good to be gotten from loving as undetachable from the activity of loving. Further, to explain why we shouldn't incessantly search for a better object of our love, we must count as a good, though not necessarily the overriding good, loyalty. Loyalty also saves Kantianism from placing us in conflict between duty and friendship. Loyalty can serve these roles for both moral systems by virtue of its being abstract enough to be a good for utilitarians and a duty for Kantians, while also tied to particular individuals—or at least it is tied to particular individuals once a relationship has been formed.

We have not completely allayed Stocker's discomfort. Stocker is also concerned with a disharmony between our desires and emotions and our duties and recognition of the good. We believe Stocker is right about this, but both utilitarianism and Kantianism tolerate it. But, we argue, they merely tolerate it rather than, as

Stocker argues, require it. We suggest that both utilitarianism and Kantianism, by virtue of focusing solely on morality, leave out judgments about people that a more complete theory of the good life, or a more complete theory of goodness of character, must address. But this issue is for another time.

References

Ryle, G. (1949). *The concept of mind.* New York: Barnes & Noble.
Stocker, M. (1976). The schizophrenia of modern ethical theories. *The Journal of Philosophy, 63/14:* 453–466.

6

In Defense of Shame

Shame in the Context of Guilt and Embarrassment

People are not built to just note and pass over their triumphs and humiliations, good deeds and sins. We care about the sort of characters we have; for this reason, a student of character must be attentive to the emotions, especially the emotions of guilt and shame (and, as we shall see, embarrassment).

In experience, guilt and shame are often fused, but we can pry them apart, analytically at least, and see the ways they relate to who we are, to the standards we apply to ourselves, and to who we want to be. To do this, we shall use our linguistic intuitions and common experience as well as data from an important series of studies by Tangney and her collaborators (Tangney, 1991; see also Gramzow & Tangney, 1992; Miller & Tangney, 1994; Niedenthal, Tangney, & Gavinski, 1994; Tangney, 1992; Tangney, Miller, Flicker, & Barlow, 1996; Tangney, Wagner, Fletcher, & Gramzow, 1992; and Tangney, Wagner, & Gramzow, 1992), but we shall come to different conclusions from hers; we shall use our disagreements as a way to articulate our position.

Words and Feelings

One might approach the question of whether and how shame, guilt, and embarrassment are distinct from the inside out or the outside in. That is, one might start with the observation that there is a unique kind of experience (phenomenology) associated with each term; one would then try to link the types of experiences with the words used to describe them and, perhaps, the situations that provoke them. Tangney and her collaborators take this approach. But we shall (usually) proceed from the other direction, from the outside in. We note that there are three different words in use in this domain, and ask: When are the different words used? In what circumstances? And, finally, in connection with what experiences?

The Difference between "Being" and "Feeling" Guilty

We start with the obvious: feeling guilty and being guilty are not the same thing. People are either guilty of transgressions or they aren't. Guilt is *not*, at first blush, the name of a feeling; it is the name of a fact about a person. Benedict Arnold was guilty of treason regardless of his feelings about the matter. Thus, to say that someone is guilty is not to comment on his current psychological state. In this way, at least, being guilty is different from being angry, afraid, jealous, envious, in love, ashamed, hungry, thirsty, sleepy, tired, bored, fed up with political rhetoric, and so on; and in this way being guilty is like being fat, pretty, smart, king, rested, in a good position to win the tournament, and so on.

But, of course, people describe themselves as *feeling guilty*. And we believe them. The question is: Does the fact that people candidly describe themselves as feeling guilty mean that there is a unique emotion (feeling)—guilt—that they are experiencing when they truthfully describe themselves as feeling guilty?

Maybe not. People do, after all, also sometimes describe themselves as feeling fat, pretty, smart, like a king, rested, in a good position to win the tournament, and so on. The English language is pretty tolerant of these things. That is, in English we are allowed to take any state-of-affairs word and convert it into a feeling term, with the reading that to feel x is to "feel the way a person who *is x* feels." So feeling like a king is a matter of feeling the way a king feels—whatever that is! But the fact that we are allowed to feel fat or like a king doesn't imply that there is some sort of unique emotional experience only fat people or kings have. The fact that we can feel guilty does not imply that there is a unique feeling of guilt, any more than the fact that we can feel like a king implies that there is a unique kingly feeling.

Let us suppose, for a moment, that *one of the ways* kings feel is proud. If this is true, are feeling like a king and feeling proud different emotions? Not really. Rather, feeling like a king is a broad term used to refer—somewhat vaguely—to any and all of the emotions kings feel (*qua* king), including proud. But this does not imply that there is a unique kingly feeling. Let us draw out the analogy to guilt.

Feeling Guilty Is Sometimes Feeling Ashamed

If feeling guilty is a matter of feeling the way a person who is guilty of something feels, then how does a guilty person feel? *One* way a guilty person feels, surely, is ashamed. On this reading, then, shame is *one* of several emotions encompassed by the broad term 'feeling guilty'. So, in a particular case a person racked by guilt might just as well be described as tormented by shame—that is, the particular guilty emotion the person is feeling is shame. This token of a guilt feeling is also, as it happens, a token of a shame feeling. This does not imply, of course, that guilt feelings are *always* shame feelings, or only shame feelings, but it allows that they may sometimes be shame feelings.

Tangney (1992), however, finds that although there is substantial overlap in what people report when asked to describe a guilt versus a shame episode, there are also reliable differences between them. For example, she finds that shame is a more intense and more intensely unpleasant emotion—a point to which we shall return; it is an emotion that involves a greater physiological jolt than does guilt; it is also less pleasant to remember.

Of course, the fact that *some* tokens of guilt are also tokens of shame is not inconsistent with Tangney's finding that subjects, on average, distinguish the two. Still, the data are compatible with our notion that 'feeling guilty' is an umbrella that collects under itself a broad range of feelings having to do with transgressions.[1]

Shame

When does a person report feeling shame (or ashamed)? To answer this, let us start with a psychological state that we will call x. (Why we call it x will, we promise, become clear.) Here's what x is: x is the state of believing that one's self has been exposed, and that that self is (in mild cases of x) unappealing, flawed, scarred; in extreme cases, the self is seen as vile, revolting, disgusting. Along with these beliefs[2] in state x is a desire in mild cases to leave, to disappear, to hide, to retreat from the world—in extreme cases, to cease to be. At the same time, in state x one feels frozen, unable to get away. Now, we propose that the description of state x we have just given is a pretty good gloss of the experience of shame; we suggest that when a person reports that she (or someone else) experienced the emotion of shame, it is this constellation of beliefs and desires that she is invoking. Tangney, similarly, characterizes shame (for the moment what we are calling state x) as a "global, painful, and devastating experience in which the self, not just behavior, is painfully scrutinized and negatively evaluated. . . . This global, negative affect is often accompanied by a sense of shrinking and being small, and by a sense of worthlessness and powerlessness. . . . Phenomenological data also suggest that shame is likely to be accompanied by a desire to hide or escape from the interpersonal situation in question" (1991, p. 599).

Feeling Ashamed versus Feeling Guilty: Moral Responsibility

This analysis of shame suggests one reason why we might have two terms—guilt and shame—even if there is only one experience. Think of someone like Nelson Rockefeller, someone who achieved quite a lot in life, eventually becoming vice-president of the United States, but who was so dyslexic he could barely read—or so the story is told. To say of Rockefeller that he felt ashamed of his inability to read (if he felt that way) is to say of him that he wanted to conceal his inability, that he believed it to be a flaw, a serious flaw, and that he would have found its revelation painful. Rockefeller might well have entered state x, have become ashamed as Tangney describes it, had his dyslexia been revealed, but we (and probably he) would not describe him as being guilty or even feeling guilty. This is so because we (and he) would not want to imply that he was (or saw himself) as *responsible* for his dyslexia. So there is good reason to distinguish shame from guilt even though both refer to flaws.

Tangney (1992) asked subjects to describe situations that produced shame or guilt and found substantial overlap between the situations producing them. She also found that situations involving failures, for example, were more likely to evoke shame than guilt. But, we argue, all failures are not the same. Some failures are failures for which people are in a moral sense responsible—they should have studied for that exam. Others are not the result of morally bad character. People shouldn't feel *guilty* about the skills they don't have and can't acquire. But even if being inept isn't one's fault, it still is a less than admirable aspect of one's self, one that a person might well conceal rather than advertise, and, hence, one apt to evoke shame.[3]

Feeling Guilty though You Aren't

The relation between feeling guilty and believing one is responsible for some wrongdoing is more complex than we have so far admitted. There are cases in which one reports guilt *feelings* even though one knows oneself not to be responsible. Let us imagine that you have (faultlessly) caused another harm (so you know you are not, in fact, guilty). Still, let us imagine that the thought of the harm you caused the other person has disrupted your sleep with feelings of sympathy for the victim, wishes you could undo the harm, and something like self-recrimination.[4] It would surely be wrong to report that you *are* guilty; that means something very different from the state of affairs we have described: to confess guilt would be to embrace responsibility.

Given your knowledge that no discrediting fact about yourself has been revealed by what happened, it would also be a bit much to report shame. But the sympathy, wish to undo, and self-recriminations are close enough to what a guilty person feels that it does make sense to report "feeling guilty" to be read as "feeling some of the discomfort that a guilty person feels." So one reason to report guilt feelings is to cover these cases in which one isn't guilty and knows it, but has some of the reactions, beliefs, and desires of a person who knows herself to be guilty. People who wake up feeling like a king don't, we propose, have (or think they have) all of the feelings that kings have; they still feel like a king, however. So too with guilt.[5]

Finally, feeling reports have a role in our self-presentations. Let us imagine that you wish to display yourself as a person of moral sensibilities. In some circumstances it is useful to report oneself as 'feeling guilty'. Reporting that one *is* guilty in a case where one obviously isn't responsible would make oneself look crazy rather then sensitive, but reporting that one *feels* guilty shows that one is so morally sensitive that one feels as if one were a guilty person even when one isn't; imagine how bad you would feel if you were guilty (cf. Goffman, 1971, on remedial interchanges)!

Summary of How Shame and Guilt Differ
(*Up to This Point*)

To review our discussion of guilt and shame so far, we have argued that:

1. Being guilty is distinct from 'feeling guilty'. Being guilty is a fact about a person and what she has done, not a fact about her psychological state.
2. 'Feeling guilty', on the other hand, allows one to assert that one is experiencing one or some of the feelings a guilty person has—including shame.
3. A person who reports that he *is* guilty in so reporting accepts responsibility for something; a person who reports being ashamed or feeling shame may fully believe that she is not responsible for what is indeed shameful.

Hence, a single term that covers shame and guilt would not suffice. 'Feeling guilty' is in one sense a broader term than 'feeling ashamed'—there are other things than shame a guilty person might feel, but 'feeling shame' is also broader than 'feeling guilty'—one might well feel shame about something that one knows oneself to be innocent of.

4. Still, a person who reports 'feeling guilty' may honestly deny that he *is* guilty and responsible, but lay claim to *some* of the criteria for the assessment of real guilt. And it is sometimes strategically useful to report guilt feelings.

Some Connections Between Guilt and Shame

A Natural Connection between Guilt and Shame

If a person knows herself to be guilty of some transgression—fully guilty—then the person must also believe that the transgression was her responsibility. But if the transgression is one for which she is fully responsible, then it followed from her decisions and, most likely, from her character, from some flawed aspect of her character. Confrontation with this aspect of one's own character is the sort of thing involved in shame. Thus, there is a natural connection between acts we are responsible for and our characters.

When Guilt and Shame Are Not Commensurate

The worse the character flaw revealed by a guilty act, the more intense the experience of shame we might expect. So there is also a connection between the intensity of the guilt feelings we might have and the shame we might also feel. Still, there are cases where the degrees of guilt and shame are not commensurate.

Imagine that a trivial failing has led, causally, to substantial harm. For example, for some people punctuality seems not to be a terribly serious matter, and being late, even chronically, isn't the sort of thing such people feel real shame about. Now suppose such a person by being five minutes late caused another to miss out on some really wonderful opportunity. Insofar as the tardy person is sure that her being late was just a reflection of this (to her) trivial flaw in her character (and not, say, envy of the other person's life of privilege), she may well feel guilty about being late—she may well focus on the bad thing that happened to her friend, wish she could make it up to her, and so on. But she can't really feel shame because she lacks the appropriate sense of how important punctuality is to the overall assessment of a person's character.[6] (But she should beware: being shameless is sometimes a shameful thing.) The assessment of the seriousness of harm done by an act and the seriousness of the character flaw revealed by an act may, therefore, differ and differ substantially; this is another reason to retain a shame-guilt distinction. Guilt is, perhaps, the more appropriate term to characterize cases in which the harm seriously exceeds the flaw; shame fits well the cases in which the flaw exceeds the harm. But this is not to deny that there are cases where the harm and the flaw are commensurate and the guilty party's experience of her guilt is one of her recognition of just how flawed she is.

Shameless Guilt: A Critique of Tangney

Tangney's research into the shame-guilt distinction seems, on the whole, consistent with the above view (1991; see also Gramzow & Tangney, 1992; Niedenthal, Tangney, & Gavinski, 1994; Tangney, 1992; Tangney, Wagner, et al., 1992; and Tangney, Wagner, & Gramzow, 1992). Yet Tangney concludes that shame is maladaptive, self-indulgent, and ego-centric, while guilt is vital to us as social beings. She presents evidence that people especially disposed to feel shame (as opposed to guilt) are likely to be especially hostile and to suffer from other pathologies (Tangney, Wagner, & Gramzow, 1992). We will argue, on the other hand, that guilt and shame in people's experience cannot be so easily segregated and that, if there were a shameless guilt, it would be anemic and unable to fulfill any important social or moral function.

Let's first review Tangney's conception of shame and guilt. For Tangney, "In guilt, the object of concern is some specific action (or failure to act). There is remorse or regret over the 'bad thing that was done' and a sense of tension that often serves as a motivation for reparative action" (Tangney, Wagner, and Gramzow, 1992, p. 469). The person who feels *ashamed,* Tangney suggests, is focusing on the self and how small and worthless he is; the person who feels guilty is focused on some specific act he did. And she has evidence that people who are focused on the guilty aspects of situations and who are asked how they would undo them think about other things they might have *done,* whereas people focused on the shameful aspect of situations focus on other things they might have *been* to undo the shame (Niedenthal et al., 1994).

So, imagine, as Niedenthal asked her subjects to imagine, a person is at a party and finds himself or herself in the following situation:

> Your good friend, who rarely dates, invites you to attend a party with him/her and his/her date, Chris. It is your friend's first date with Chris. You go along and discover that Chris is not only very attractive, but is flirting with you. You flirt back. Although you are not seriously interested in him/her, at the end of the night you give Chris your phone number. The next day your good friend raves to you about how much he/she liked Chris (Niedenthal et al., 1994, p. 591).

Tangney's hypothesis was that there were two possible reactions to this scenario:

1. The subjects might focus on undoing what the protagonist did (for instance, on having given Chris the phone

number, on how bad the situation is for the dateless friend, and on how the protagonist might call Chris up and tell Chris that he's not interested in her romantically—he had actually given her his phone number strictly in the hope that she was an insurance salesperson and would call up to discuss his added coverage, and, anyway, he is joining the French Foreign Legion tomorrow, and that every witty thing he had said the day before was actually written by, and passed to him, by his best friend). Focusing on the protagonist's action, his friend's sad state, and trying to fix the situation are all, on Tangney's analysis, aspects of feeling guilty.

2. But one might, on the other hand, think about the fact that the protagonist's stealing Chris from his best friend shows that he is a worm. So, alternatively, the subjects might focus on what a selfish, sneaky, impulsive, miserable excuse for a human he is. That sort of reaction is, according to Tangney, shame. (It is, a powerful, unpleasant emotion, one that might motivate you to keep your number to yourself the next time a Chris appears.[7])

And the investigators found, subjects did tend to focus on one or the other depending on whether they were thinking about guilt or shame.

We are worried about the first reaction, the one Tangney calls guilt. It doesn't seem to be much of an emotion, and if it is an emotion, it isn't clear it is guilt. To be guilty, or for that matter to feel guilty, is to have a very special involvement in some situation. But you needn't have that special involvement to have the concern Tangney assigns to the guilty person. You don't have to be guilty of flirting, for example, to feel sorry for your best friend or to want to fix the situation. Suppose that you learned that your friend Pat had been doing the flirting with Chris and had stolen Chris from your other friend TJ; you might feel very sorry for TJ, wish the situation were different, wish you could undo Pat's actions, and feel tempted to call Chris up and explain what a rat Pat is and what a wonderful person TJ is (thus fulfilling all of Tangney's criteria for feeling guilty). If Tangney is correct about what feeling guilty is—that is, an amalgam of sympathy for the victim and a desire to undo the situation—then it seems that you can feel guilty over things you had nothing to do with. But most of us wouldn't say that the empathic, morally sensitive onlooker was feeling guilty!

We suggest that the experience of pure guilt *as Tangney defines it* is at most a fairly mild emotion; intense guilt—Rodion Romanavitch Raskolnokov guilt—*that* guilt, we suggest, has as its bite shame. Tangney's analysis too thoroughly dissociates shame from guilt, character from action. Acts for which we are guilty (and don't just in some weak sense feel guilty) do involve the self. And because they involve the self, they involve shame.

Shame and Voluntarism

Tangney would like to replace shame with guilt; shame is an untherapeutic emotion. Her rejection of shame reflects the values of our voluntarist culture: our culture believes that a person should be judged by the choices he or she has made, by his or her decisions. Shame, something that can strike the innocent, is anathema to this core belief.[8]

Guilt (by itself, devoid of shame) just doesn't hurt enough. It may just be true about human beings that shame is an excruciating emotion, that facing our moral depravity may be as painful as facing disfigurement in the mirror. It may be horrible enough an experience to get people to do (or give up) quite a lot to avoid it,[9] even face death—even certain death—rather than see themselves as cowards. On the other hand, it might be that the anticipation that if you do x you will wish you hadn't done x and wish you could restore the situation to the status quo ante—guilt devoid of shame—just isn't powerful enough to counter serious temptation. Tangney (1992, 1995) has data, as we have mentioned, that suggest that shame is a more painful emotion than guilt.

Character

On consideration, strict voluntarism would seem to be an impossible basis for a moral order, or even for a coherent personality—after all, character *itself* isn't chosen.[10] So if what is important about us is what we *do*, what we choose, and if character is something we are, not something we do, then why is *it* important? Why should I feel ashamed of my traits of character—even if those traits led to evil outcomes—since I didn't choose those traits in the first place? So it is not merely shame but character as well that is incompatible with a voluntarist society.

There is even a practical, educational psychotherapeutic reason that we can't do without shame. Bad character needs to be nipped in the bud *before* seriously bad things happen. If the very decision as to what is a good and a bad trait of character depends on outcomes—actual outcomes the way guilt does—then we can't decide that Joe's greed is a bad thing until it has gotten Joe into trouble. (And, worse, Joe can't react in horror to his greed when he first sees it.) But we might hope that Joe's shame (and pride) would be involved earlier, at the first outcroppings of his greed *before* he had anything to feel guilty about. So, Tangney's program for the abolition of shame is not merely impossible but imprudent.

Shame and Guilt in Cultural Context

As Tangney (1996) has pointed out, there is a third position about the relation of guilt to shame; Ruth Benedict (1946) famously proposed that Japanese culture was a shame culture while European and American (Anglo) culture was a guilt culture (Cf. Mead, 1971). Guilt cultures, the story goes, rely on an internalized sense of right and wrong to control behavior; shame cultures, on the other hand, rely on people's concerns about how they look to others. America, it was alleged, is home for a culture in which people do what they should—insofar as they do what they should—because of this internalized sense of right and wrong. Japan, it was alleged, houses a culture in which people do what they should—insofar as they do what they should—because of their desires to have themselves and their families look good in the eyes of others. We might succumb to social psychologists' favorite metaphor and say that American culture is one in which people are internally controlled, while Japanese culture is one in which they are externally controlled.

Now Benedict, in fact, saw the difference between these cultures as a matter of degree and emphasis, *not* as a categorical difference Benedict (1946), although the popularization of her view makes this simplistic contrast (cf. Piers & Singer, 1953). She did *not* assert that America had guilt but no shame while Japan had shame but no guilt. Still, it is instructive to see what she could have meant had she asserted that Japan was a pure shame culture while America was a pure guilt culture.

To appreciate this distinction, first imagine, if you will, someone who was caught doing something that he does not believe to be morally wrong in the slightest, but that he knows that other people believe to be so. Would such a person describe his experience as one of shame? Imagine, for example, someone from a culture without a menstrual taboo visiting a culture with one; if he were known to have slept with his wife during the menses, would he feel ashamed? Would he report being ashamed? If he did, could there be better evidence that he had "gone native," had internalized the culture's values? (Of course, he might refrain from mentioning what had happened out of a variety of concerns. He might not want to shock his informants, or lose esteem in their eyes, or whatever.) So if one has not internalized some aspect of a behavioral code, then being caught violating that code can't produce authentic shame.

Second, imagine that in some culture it is widely known that no one has internalized anything; it is a pure shame culture (in Benedict's sense) and known to be such. But shame, at the very least, on this account requires that people think other people look down on them, look upon them as flawed. But in this pure shame culture, why would people think that anyone else would see them as flawed? If it is well known that there are no internalized standards of behavior or character, then there is no internalized sense that some people are flawed. A culture without internalized standards is a culture without *guilt or shame*.[11]

Another way that it has been popular to construe Benedict's guilt-shame distinction is that shame requires an audience while guilt doesn't. But the Miller and Tangney (1994) data suggest that, at least for our culture, people can feel shame even when alone (see also Tangney, 1995; Tangney, Miller, et al., 1996). So shame does not require an audience. We agree with Tangney that Joseph Conrad's Lord Jim is ashamed of himself for having jumped ship, and he experiences that shame whenever he thinks about this sad incident from his past whether he is alone or with others. Yet most of us experience an emotion akin to shame that *is* dependent on an audience.

Shame and Embarrassment

We promised at the outset of this chapter to distinguish guilt, shame, and embarrassment. We owe now a treatment of embarrassment and a justification for why we should treat embarrassment alongside shame and guilt (Cf. Miller & Tangney, 1994). In our discussion above of the mental state of shame, we referred to the state not as shame but as state x; why did we employ this state x artifice? Isn't state x just shame by another name?

It isn't just shame, we suggest, because it is also embarrassment; that is, the characterization we have given of state x is compatible with state x's being embarrassment as well as with its being shame. To see this, imagine that just as you are about to walk down the aisle in your tuxedo at your wedding your clumsy best man spills the glass of tomato juice he is drinking on your white shirt. We suggest that the reaction to this event might well be that you enter into state x.

A sensible third party describing your experience of state x (and you yourself describing it at some other time and place) would surely describe you as embarrassed, not ashamed. There is a good reason for this choice. We suggest that in using the term 'shame' a speaker, whether speaking in the first person or the third, commits herself to the claim that the fact about character revealed by the state-x-provoking-event is *in fact* discrediting, or, at least, is so thought by the person experiencing the emotion. Describing oneself (or another) as embarrassed, on the other hand, makes no such claim and may even suggest that state x (as it is in this case) is not really the result of a discrediting fact about one's character.[12]

So we make the following suggestion: when one knows one is the center of attention, one enters into this state—state x—which involves the feeling of exposure[13] and the experience of being flustered, confused, out of play. In some cases, one may fully believe that a terrible self is being revealed, in which case one may—quite literally—want to die, and one would describe oneself as ashamed or experiencing shame. At the other extreme, one may believe that though everyone's attention is on a flaw—the tomato juice stain—it isn't really a flaw of one's own character, *though one can certainly see how the audience might think it such a flaw* (unless one focuses on what one's character must be to have picked this guy as best man).

Still, the red stain is, at the very least, a dramaturgic flaw, a hurdle, an obstruction to the smooth performance of one's role, something that could cause one to become flustered, frustrated, and want to retreat, flee, or get the damned thing over with (Goffman, 1956). And, of course, the more rooted the audience's attention is on the flaw, the harder it is to create (or re-create) the character one was supposed to be performing—a groom should be a figure of dignity, at least for his moment on the stage. So the more attentive to the flaw the audience becomes the more flustered one becomes. This, too, can be a very painful state, but one that surely one would describe as embarrassment and not shame.

Of course, there are lots of cases in life in which it isn't at all clear just what the flaw is that is being revealed. One can understand how a wedding night malfunction might seem *at the time* to reveal something terribly discrediting. But then again it might not. Is the person ashamed or embarrassed on his wedding night? How would he describe it then? Isn't that up for grabs? Surely if all goes well the following morning, then embarrassment is the right word. But if things never go well, then we are set for an appearance on *Geraldo* to ward off shame. Of course, any empirical inquiry that asks people retrospectively to report instances of embarrassment will lead them to pick examples that are clearly *just* embarrassing. But it might be a mistake to read the clarity that distance and revolution provide into the experience *as it unfolded*.

Our suggestion, then, is that the experience of shame and the experience of embarrassment share many features. In both cases, one has a sense of being exposed. In both cases, a flaw is revealed. In the case of shame, it is a flaw in the actor's character that is revealed; in the case of embarrassment, it is a flaw in the character that is being enacted. Thus, it is the groom in this story who *no matter how painful the event was at the time* is likely to tell the story of the tomato juice with real pleasure in the future. The best man is much less likely to do so—though, we suggest, they were both in considerable distress at the time of the event. Both were in the evolving state x.[14]

Conclusion

We have argued that shame ill fits our voluntarist culture. People, as Tangney points out, can be ashamed of things that they did not chose, that they did not will, that aren't their fault. This strikes us as unfair.[15] If the only grounds allowed for praising or condemning people are moral, then it really is unfair. And our experiencing shame seems a flaw; being shameless seems a virtue—contrary to what our mothers told us. But moral grounds are not the only grounds we have for praising or condemning people. We, after all, value beauty, intelligence, and strength of character—even sometimes in those who use that character in a way we find immoral. The fact that we value these qualities suggests that just as we make aesthetic judgments about much of our world, we make aesthetic judgments about character—our own and other people's. Positive aesthetic judgments about ourselves result in pride; less favorable ones in shame (see chapter 2, for a discussion). It is a fatal corruption of *moral* judgment if it be unfair; it is no flaw at all of aesthetic judgment if it be unfair—the beauty of a painting (or its lack) is surely independent of the effort of its creator.

Tangney's position suggests that shame is an irrational and destructive emotion, one we would be better off without. Seen as we suggest it should be seen—as a fundamentally aesthetic response to our judgments of our character—it is no more (or less) irrational than our appreciation of beauty and ugliness more generally.

We have suggested, too, that without the bite of shame, guilt lacks force. We have suggested that what keeps many of us from doing things the world is better off without our doing is not guilt but this very shame Tangney wishes to relieve us of.

Notes

1. Tangney (1995) says that guilt is sometimes used as a catch-all term in this way. The difference between us is, perhaps, that she believes that there is a precise, narrow, proper use for 'feeling guilty' that picks out a unique feeling state, but that 'guilt feelings' can also be used in a less principled, more general way. We think that 'guilt feelings' can only be used in a general way. There is a legitimate place in our language of relationships not only for "maternal-third-cousin-once-removed" but also for "relative."

2. We use here the strong term 'believe'; in so doing, we march in where tip-toeing is the far better policy. Consider three cases. You are caught with your hand in the cookie jar. You believe you are exposed, and you believe a fact of your character (gluttony) has been exposed. A second case: You deliberately and politically decide to "come out" as a whatever. You certainly know you are exposed, but you do not believe that what has been exposed is discrediting *or that those who think so have any right to think so*. Here you believe (rightly) you are exposed, but not that your self is in fact discredited. The third case: You ask a stranger on the subway for his seat as a class assignment (see Milgram & Sabini, 1978). You believe (rightly) you are the center of attention and you believe (rightly) that others are at least suspicious of your character. And you believe (rightly) that, given what they see, they are entitled to that belief. And you believe (rightly) that you aren't exactly in control of this situation. Now, case 1 fits our analysis of state x fully. Case 2 we would reject as a state x example. But we would embrace case 3 as a state x example *even though* this is a case in which one doesn't *believe* that a tainted self is being revealed. So *belief* is too strong, but we have no word to take its place.

3. Tangney, Miller, et al. (1996) did *not*, however, find differences between shame and guilt in terms of moral responsibility. Can we reconcile that finding with our claim? Well, certainly, post hoc we can! We would suggest that the shameful things *one has done* are actually less humiliating than the shameful things one *is* and has no control over. One may be ashamed of having cheated on one's wife, but at

least one can promise not to do it again. But what can one do about being schizophrenic? Perhaps subjects asked to provide things they felt shame over picked things they had control over and, thus, as it happened, also picked things they were morally responsible for and felt guilty about. Looking for the less shameful things they could report, they hit on their moral rather than their aesthetic failings (cf. Silver, Conte, Miceli, & Poggi, 1986).

4. A delicate matter: if one believes the recriminations one is making against oneself, then there are grounds to feel shame. But making recriminations and believing them are different. The suggestion here is that people are sometimes more willing to entertain self-recriminations than they are to believe them true. In this sense, they feel guilty even though they conclude in the end that they are not.

5. We suspect that people are most likely to feel guilty, though they are blameless, if they can imagine something they could have done or not done—"if they had only known"—to prevent the mishap (cf. Kahneman & Tversky, 1982, on the simulation heuristic). If they are in the *causal chain* leading to the mishap, this sort of guilt is most likely—e.g., if you bought a ticket to Paris as a birthday present for your mother on TWA 800, on its fatal flight. We also suspect that when people feel guilty in this sort of situation they are actually able to find some far-fetched responsibility to have done, or have not done, something: an irrational guilt is driven by an irrational responsibility.

6. Of course, things aren't really this simple. This token of lack of punctuality is also a token of lack of consideration. And while lack of punctuality may be to our heroine a trivial failing, lacking consideration of others may be a more serious failing. So which flaw of character does this token display? As every labeling theorist reminded us, it is hard to say.

7. We certainly agree that the latter reaction, feeling like a worm, is one of shame. Isn't this reaction *also* one of guilt? If you learned that this was the contents of the consciousness—i.e., I am a worm—of the second person and were asked, Does that person feel guilty? would you answer no?

8. A measure, albeit a flawed one, of our culture's aversion to shame as a central moral emotion is afternoon talk television. Afternoon talk television is populated, it seems, by people who our mothers would have described (indifferently) as lacking shame or lacking pride,

telling us the most horrible facts about themselves seemingly without pain.

9. Tangney's (Tangney, Wagner, Hill-Barlow, & Marschall, 1996) data show that *having done something wrong,* people who feel guilt (unmarked by shame) are more likely to respond to their victim in a helpful way than are people who feel shame. That, surely, is a leg up for guilt over shame. But the social order, one imagines, cannot survive unless people *avoid* doing lots of things they might want to do. We are arguing not about how people who are currently feeling shame or who are currently 'feeling guilty' might act, but about what people might do to *avoid* these states.

10. Sometimes it is 'chosen'. It may be, as Aristotle argued, that there comes a point when an addict can no longer control her behavior in the face of her addiction. Neither her actions nor her character are open to choice *at this point*. But there may have been a point where she could have chosen to resist; *at that point* she, as it were, chose this character. Still much of character is, we suppose, never chosen.

11. Of course, one can imagine a culture in which no one has internalized anything, but everyone believes that everyone else has. In that culture, we understand why people would think that others would look down on them, but this is a culture in which no one is really ashamed of anything. Rather, it is a culture in which people are prudently eager to conceal certain facts about themselves because it would be difficult for them if the facts were to leak out. This isn't a shame culture, it is a hypocrisy culture. (One can only speculate about how long such a culture could last before the secret got out.)

12. Compare this argument with Tangney, Miller, et al.'s (1996) finding that shame and guilt are more closely tied to morality than is embarrassment; we would argue that it is character failings—certainly including moral ones—to which shame is tied.

13. We take the view that embarrassment requires an audience, though shame does not. We are discussing here, then, all cases of embarrassment and some cases of shame.

14. Thus, for us, shame and embarrassment aren't necessarily distinct emotional states as experiences; for Tangney they are.

15. Of course, sometimes even though something is unchosen in the first place, it comes to have a strong connection to the person. Friends, for example, are often unchosen in any developed sense. Yet

we become loyal to our friends; they become part of us. Ethnicity is unchosen, yet for some people, at least, it is an important part of who they are. Aspects of character, though often unchosen, may like ethnicity be embraced.

References

Benedict, R. (1946). *The chrysanthemum and the sword: Patterns of Japanese culture*. Boston: Houghton-Mifflin.

Goffman, E. (1956). Embarrassment and social organization. *American Journal of Sociology, 62*, 264–271.

Goffman, E. (1971). *Relations in Public*. New York: Harper.

Gramzow, R., & Tangney, J. P. (1992). Proneness to shame and the narcissistic personality. *Personality & Social Psychology Bulletin, 18*, 369–376.

Kahneman, D., & Tversky, A. (1982). The simulation heuristic. In D. Kahneman, P. Slovic, & A. Tversky (Eds.), *Judgments under uncertainty*. New York: Cambridge University Press.

Mead, M. (1971). Some anthropological considerations concerning guilt. In R. W. Smith (Ed.), *Guilt, men, and society*. New York: Anchor.

Milgram, S., & Sabini, J. (1978). On maintaining urban norms: A field experiment in the subway. In A. Baum, J. E. Singer, & S. Valins (Eds.), *Advances in environmental psychology, Vol. 1* (pp. 31–40). Hillsdale, N.J.: Erlbaum.

Miller, R. S., & Tangney, J. P. (1994). Differentiating embarrassment and shame. *Journal of Social & Clinical Psychology, 13*, 273–287.

Niedenthal, P. M., Tangney, J. P., & Gavanski, I. (1994). "If only I weren't" versus "If only I hadn't": Distinguishing shame and guilt in conterfactual thinking. *Journal of Personality & Social Psychology, 67*, 585–595.

Piers, G., & Singer, M. B. (Eds.). (1953). *Shame and guilt: a psychoanalytic and a cultural study*. Springfield, IL: Thomas.

Silver, M., Conte, R., Miceli, M., & Poggi, I. (1986). Humiliation: Feelings, social control, and the construction of an identity. *Journal for the Theory of Social Behaviour, 16*, 269–285.

Tangney, J. P. (1991). Moral affect: The good, the bad, and the ugly. *Journal of Personality & Social Psychology, 61*, 598–607.

Tangney, J. P. (1992). Situational determinants of shame and guilt in young adulthood. *Personality & Social Psychology Bulletin, 18,* 199–206.

Tangney, J. P. (1995). Recent advances in the empirical study of shame and guilt. *American Behavioral Scientist, 38,* 1132–1145.

Tangney, J. P., Hill-Barlow, D., Wagner, P. E., & Marschall, D. E. (1996). Assessing individual differences in constructive versus destructive responses to anger across the lifespan. *Journal of Personality & Social Psychology, 70,* 780–796.

Tangney, J. P., Miller, R. S., Flicker, L., & Barlow, D. H. (1996). Are shame, guilt, and embarrassment distinct emotions? *Journal of Personality & Social Psychology, 70,* 1256–1269.

Tangney, J. P., Wagner, P., Fletcher, C., & Gramzow, R. (1992). Shamed into anger? The relation of shame and guilt to anger and self-reported aggression. *Journal of Personality & Social Psychology, 62,* 669–675.

Tangney, J. P., Wagner, P., & Gramzow, R. (1992). Proneness to shame, proneness to guilt, and psychopathology. *Journal of Abnormal Psychology, 101,* 469–478.

Tangney, J. P., Wagner, P. E., Hill-Barlow, D., Marschall, D. E. (1996). Relation of shame and guilt to constructive versus destructive responses to anger across the lifespan. *Journal of Personality & Social Psychology, 70,* 797–809.

7

On Knowing Self-Deception

People sometimes say that they saw a unicorn. But unicorns don't exist. They did see something, however. If they had been at a circus, they probably saw a goat's horn glued to a colt's forehead; if they had been on an African plain, they probably glimpsed a svelte rhino at a considerable distance. In either case, their claims were illusory; they were not talking about what they thought they were talking about.

People sometimes say that they've noticed someone deceiving herself. Or they might say: "If she believed that, then she was fooling herself"; "Don't kid yourself about him"; "He just couldn't face the truth, so he lied to himself"; "She didn't want to know." Some scholars suspect that these claims are like reports of unicorn sightings and that self-deception is no more prevalent than genuine unicorns. People notice something, but that something isn't 'self-deception'. In this view, when people talk about self-deception they are unwittingly referring to cases of either deceit or error. Canfield and Gustavson (1962), for instance, argue that what is called self-deception is really a matter of having a belief in "belief-adverse" circumstances—an odd or surprising mistake.[1]

Self-deception looks mysterious, paradoxical, like a conceptual unicorn because it doesn't seem possible to deceive yourself and be deceived. As the deceiver you have to know that you are hiding something from someone. But as the deceived you cannot, conceptually cannot, know what is hidden—or else you are not deceived (this is the paradox that Sartre, 1943/1982, celebrated).

We agree that fooling oneself is quite a trick, as mysterious as, to steal Champlain's example (1977), how it's possible to strangle oneself (since as you pass out you release your grip). But strangling oneself is not paradoxical; it just requires a few props and a little knowledge of physiology. We think that something similar is true of deceiving yourself—a few props and a little cognitive psychology.

But why bother analyzing self-deception? Does the concept capture something important missed by 'error' or 'deceit'? Let's imagine a story and see what differences, if any, there are in interpreting the action as revolving around deceit, error, or self-deception.

A loving father notices that his normally ebullient daughter is becoming more and more withdrawn, listless, and grouchy. She loses her appetite. She gets calls at odd hours and then leaves the house abruptly, yet her old friends don't stop by anymore. She starts wearing long-sleeved blouses even though it's summer and refuses to go to the beach, once her favorite spot. She begins to lock her room, something she rarely used to do. He occasionally asks if she's feeling all right, but she dismisses him with a laconic "yeah." One day she is discovered dead with a needle in her arm. When the police tell him the news, he says that he can't believe that his daughter was a junkie, that he is dumbfounded, that it's all impossible.

What can we make of the father's reaction? Perhaps he is feigning for the police. He might have known about his daughter, but pretended that he didn't. After all, disclosure could be dangerous. On the other hand, his surprise might be genuine. He might be obtuse about signs of drug use.

Both of these interpretations account for parts of our story but leave other parts puzzling. If the father really knew his daughter was a junkie, and if he loved his daughter, then why hadn't he acted? A loving father acts in such a situation. He must not have known. But how could a loving father, one who cares about his daughter's welfare, see all the signs that something was wrong and yet not think about them, even for a moment? How could he fail even to investigate? He must have known something. When we start from a deceit account we veer to ignorance, and when we start from ignorance we veer to deceit. That is one reason that we want an account like self-deception, one that holds a place for both.

Further, our reaction to the father is probably a mix of contempt and censure on one hand—"sure he's really surprised"—and pity on the other; we empathize with his suffering. Our reaction, in other words, seems to be a blend of reactions to someone who was innocently ignorant and to someone who is deceiving us. Once again a notion like self-deception appears to be needed.

There is one further observation we will squeeze from this story. The father's "ignorance" seems to derive from the same motive that he has for deceit, that is, avoiding the embarrassment of having to admit that his daughter was a junkie. If the father didn't care whether his daughter was a junkie or not, then he would have realized that she was one. So in this story, ignorance and deception (or rather, the motives for each) appear to be linked. These are reasons to interpret this soap opera as a tale of self-deception and not merely one of error or deceit. Still, if the notion of self-deception is incoherent, our only recourse will be to construct the story in terms of deception or error. Is it incoherent?

Why Deceiving Oneself Isn't Self-Contradictory

Let us examine an important objection to the coherence of self-deception—that it is impossible for the same person to deceive and be deceived; that is, the deceiver must know what he is deceiving about and the deceived can't know it. But is it true that the deceiver must know what the deceived is in error about?

Consider: As part of a murder plot I mis-set all of the clocks in your house to deceive you into thinking it is later than it is. You look at one of these clocks and it says 8:30, but it isn't. You are deceived as to what time it is; I did the deceiving, but *I don't necessarily know what time it is.* Perhaps, as it happens, my own watch has stopped, so I haven't the foggiest idea what time it is at this very moment. But, as it happens, I also don't care. (The plot works by getting you to take a second dose of a drug too soon after the first. As long as I know you will do that, I have no need to know what time it really is!) Now in this case someone is deceived about something—led to believe something that isn't true—by someone else, but as it happens, the deceiver doesn't know the truth of the matter about which the first person is deceived. But, one might argue, the deceiver does know *something* the deceived doesn't know: that the pigeon has been had. Indeed! But each point in its time. For the moment we promised to show only that you don't need to know the right answer to deceive someone else about it.

Now having got this far it is easy enough to show that one can deceive oneself. We know lots of people who do it in just the way we have described; they mis-set their own alarm clocks to get themselves to work on time. The trick works because the person reading the clock in the befogged state of just awakening either forgets that the clock has been mis-set, or knows it has been mis-set, *but does not know just how much.* Now we are *not* suggesting that this is a good example of what people would want to call self-deception. It isn't, and we shall presently get on to why it isn't. *But* it is a perfectly fine example of a person's deceiving herself, and *that* is one of the ways that self-deception is supposed to be self-contradictory. (Another such example is Champlain's camouflage expert taken in by one of his own artifacts; see Champlain, 1977, for other examples to this point.)

So far, if we have succeeded in what we set out to do, we have convinced you that a person need not know the fact of the matter in order to deceive another about it, and that a person can deceive herself. We have begged, for the moment, the issues that surround knowing *that* one has deceived. We have also left you with an example of a person's deceiving herself that isn't a case of self-deception; now we turn to why it isn't.

WHY SOME DECEPTIONS WORKED ON ONESELF AREN'T SELF-DECEPTIONS

A plausible reason to not see the alarm clock mis-setting as an example of self-deception is that there is nothing wrong (in a moral sense) with doing it. Self-deception would seem to require doing something wrong (Lineham, 1982, for instance, sees culpability as criterial for 'self-deception'). The father in our initial story, for example, did do something wrong; he did not offer his daughter the help that she needed (and he could have given), and so he failed in his duty as a father. It therefore seems that what distinguishes instances of deceiving oneself that are genuinely 'self-deception' from those that aren't is that we call deceiving oneself self-deception if, and only if, the deceiving is morally tainted. This might be right, but it isn't. We shall argue that morally transgressing is not criterial for 'self-deception' (in the way that it is, say, for envy; Sabini & Silver, 1982, chap. 2). Still, engaging in self-deception does say something interesting about character—a point we will turn to at the end of this chapter.

Consider: You are a cocaine runner. You have inadvertently

learned the name of your supplier. You are afraid that if the police get you, you will spill the name. And you believe that this would be regrettable—the mob isn't very understanding about such matters. So you take yourself to a hypnotist to make yourself the 'victim' of misinformation. Fortunately, the hypnosis is a success, and you now sincerely believe that the name of your supplier is Ronald Reagan. Would we call this self-deception? We think not. Rather, this story seems to be more like the case of mis-setting your own alarm clock—a case in which you have deceived yourself, but not an example of what people call self-deception. But the reason we don't see this as self-deception is *not* that we see protecting mob big shots as morally ennobling. Rather, we suggest the grounds of withholding the characterization of 'self-deception' lay elsewhere.

WHICH DECEPTIONS OF SELF ARE 'SELF-DECEPTIONS'?

To be guilty of 'self-deception,' we propose, someone must deceive himself for a specific kind of reason. Self-deception involves deceiving oneself in order to manipulate one's feelings. More specifically, the psychological state must be the ultimate, rather than intermediate, goal of the manipulation. In the previous examples of deceiving oneself, examples that intuitively weren't instances of self-deception, the deceiver has manipulated her psychological state all right, but in order to achieve something else, a pragmatic goal—get to work on time or to save her life. There are two kinds of reasons, then, to manipulate one's feelings: the first is to be better able to achieve things in the world; the second is to control the feelings per se. As we have illustrated, deceiving oneself for the first sort of reason isn't self-deception; deceiving oneself for the second is.

Why would one bother to manipulate one's psychological state for its own sake? It makes sense to do this because we happen to be creatures who have emotions; that is, we are creatures who react to our beliefs about the world in two different kinds of ways. One way is to operate on the world so as to change it (or keep it from becoming unpleasant). The second way is to experience emotions. Thus, to know that someone we love has died or left us may make us feel sad, to know that a tiger is chasing us may make us feel afraid, to know that we have failed may make us feel ashamed, to know that we have succeeded may make us proud, and so on. These feelings that come in the wake of beliefs, then, are painful or pleasant of themselves, and we might, then, want to produce them or prevent them, independent of our desire to produce the states of affairs in the world that they refer to.[2]

If we wanted to show that the father of the junkie was deceiving himself, we would point out ways that he acted to preserve his feelings of tranquility, avoid feelings of shame, and so on, as a primary goal, and that his doing so led him to misunderstand what was happening to his daughter.[3]

In this view, to set the alarm clock fast in order to trick oneself in getting to work on time isn't self-deception, but to set the clock *slow*, to produce the soothing feeling that one is on time when one isn't, *is* self-deception. This idea of 'self-deception' allows us to distinguish it from some other kinds of beliefs, especially faith.

Why Faith Isn't Self-Deception

Gardner (1970) convincingly argues that beliefs in the teeth of the evidence—such as in the "second coming" or in the "just revolution"—superficially appear to be self-deceptive, but need not be. How is such faith different from self-deception? One way it is different, Gardner argues, is that his opposition to the reasonable is recognized, even affirmed—*credo quia absurdum*. We think that the more important reason that faith isn't, or, rather, need not be, self-deception is that it does not have, or need not have, a psychological state as its object.

Suppose a person believed in a God even though he knew that there was no reason to do so. Is this self-deception? Well, it might be. The Freudian argument, for example, is that belief in God is driven by a fear of facing the fact that there is no one who can be counted on to make things right. On the Freudian view, then, we invent God in order to comfort ourselves, and this is, on our account, self-deception—even if we also recognize that our belief has an odd status. But suppose you believed in a God because only if there is a God can people truly be kin, or, more selfishly, only with a God can there be an afterlife, something you desire. Is this self-deception? We think not. Your believe here is not held to manipulate your own psychological state. Your belief may be foolish, but that's a different story. Loyalty to a friend may also motivate this sort of belief, this sort of faith, but insofar as it isn't motivated by a desire to manipulate one's psychological state, it isn't self-deception. (See Sabini & Silver, 1989, for more on loyalty.)

The Real Mystery of Self-Deception

In the story of the mis-set alarm clock we showed that it is possible to deceive oneself about what time it is. But we noted that there was another deception involved in this story: the deception about deceiving oneself. We begged the question of the role of that second deception. But it is now time to face the problem that the person as 'deceiver' must also deceive himself as 'victim' about the fact of the deception (see Fingarette, 1969, for more on the issue of double deception). This second deception is harder to arrange. In the clock example, the deceiving of oneself works only because the 'victim' is groggy in the morning and thus forgets the prior evening's deception. This example works by a cheap trick, one making use of a temporary and rather restricted weakness. The trick was useful in showing that there was no conceptual incoherence in the notion of 'self-deception,' but it certainly didn't shed much light on how self-deception might ordinarily work. Can better examples of self-deception be constructed? Can we be aware of our fudging the facts and still deceive ourselves?

COOKED EVIDENCE

One is seriously tempted to answer this question, "No." But this is a temptation one does well to resist. The impression that one has to forget that one cooked the evidence in order to be affected by it relies on the assumption that we are never manipulated by evidence we know to be cooked. But, in fact, we *can* be manipulated by evidence we know is cooked. Advertisers make their living by manipulating us in just this way. There is even experimental evidence that people remain persuaded of things despite having been explicitly told that the very thing they have been persuaded of has been made up (Ross, Lepper, & Hubbard, 1975). If we can be persuaded by other people who we know are tampering with the data, why should we not be able to persuade ourselves when we tamper with data? We now want to consider some ways that people fail to notice how much they have been affected by evidence that they know to have been altered.

To see that someone can be persuaded by a case he knows to be one-sided, imagine you are the father of the drug addict we have been discussing. And imagine a trial of your daughter before a jury in which you are to play the role of defense attorney. The trial is to be a special one, one in which the facts that triggered your suspicion that she was taking drugs are allowed into evidence for the prosecution, but from that point on the prosecutor doesn't get to make a case; you, the defense attorney, and you alone, are allowed to speak. Is this likely to be a fair trial? Is it likely to lead to the right verdict? Would an unbiased jury have the evidence necessary to render a fair verdict? The jury would realize, of course, that you were biased and would take that into account. But this still does not amount to a fair trial. If only your daughter's side of the story were told, how could the jury know how much to discount it? How would they know the strength of the case the prosecutor could have made? Of course, no real court would allow such a procedure. Real judges know that reminders to the jury that the defense is biased are no substitute for a prosecution's case.

The point of this story and metaphor is that thinking about something can be profitably conceived of as two distinct activities: presenting evidence to ourselves and reaching a judgment on the basis of the evidence.[4] There are, then, two corresponding ways a person in self-deception might be biased—in presenting evidence to herself and in judging that evidence. It is easy enough to see how deception would be the outcome if the jury, the person making the judgment, were biased. But to posit bias in the judging person—or judgmental faculty—is, as Sartre saw, to beg the question of how self-deception works. For how can the deceived party be biased in just the right way to avoid knowing the truth unless she knows the truth? Thus we don't want to explain self-deception by positing bias on the part of the judging faculty.

But there is no question begging involved in positing bias on the part of the presenter of the evidence; the presenter of the facts need know only the case she is trying to make, she need not believe in that case for her presentation to be effective. Thus we want to show that deception can result with a deceptive attorney, but an unbiased jury. Insofar as an unbiased jury would be persuaded, then all of the bias has been loaded onto the presenter of the case. And if all of the bias can be located there, then self-deception has been explained.

Let us apply our courtroom metaphor now to the father's psychology. He notices some disquieting fact about his daughter. Since the fact is disquieting, and since he does not wish to explode his peace and quiet, he, as deceiver, sets out to make the "best case" for his daughter. But he is also the juror. Since he is one person, he knows that his presentation of the evidence is biased, so he discounts it—a bit. But he doesn't discount it enough. He has now been deceived—not because he has forgotten that he has been trying to deceive but because, even though he knew he has been one-sidedly presenting (or spelling out, to use Fingarette's term) the case, it still looks compelling. The father is in the role of both jury and defense attorney. His desire to know the truth about his daughter in order to help her makes him like a juror—indeed, an unbiased juror. On the other hand, his natural inclination to be loyal to his daughter, and his equally natural inclination not to start a fuss, turns him into a defense attorney. The point is that there are two distinct roles that one person can play. One person can pull off both roles because the fact that the juror can listen in on the defense's strategy does not make this strategy pointless (although it may make it less effective).[5] Of course, you can't make a silk purse out of a sow's ear. You can't fit any facts to any story. If the case against the daughter is compelling enough, and the father still won't face the facts, then he isn't engaged in self-deception, he is crazy.

Your knowledge that you are cooking the data, then, does not preclude your being influenced by your cooking, though it does make it harder. Any way that you can reduce the salience or apparent importance of the data tampering, making it seem incidental and not essential, should make the cooking more appetizing. Of course, some cases are easier to tamper with unobtrusively than are others.

For instance, if the argument you wish to present is easy to make, then it will seem as if you're not doing much fudging at all. If it is very hard, then it will be harder to ignore your bias. Using how difficult it is to make a case as a sign of how unlikely the case is to be true sounds like a good guide to finding the truth, but it isn't. Let us return to the courtroom to see why.

Note that in the court of your own mind, there are *two* key figures missing—the prosecutor and the judge. One important role judges play is to rule on the probative value of evidence. They disallow evidence that is more persuasive than it ought to be; they disallow evidence that stirs up the emotions to a degree that would interfere with a juror's rational assessment of the evidence. Jurors might be unbiased, but they do have emotions. And playing on these emotions can produce distortions in judgment. Hence, certain kinds of arguments and displays of evidence are not allowed. As the maker of a case for your own consumption you need honor no such constraints. You may be able to make a compelling case even though it is not very likely to be true. But if you, now as the perfectly unbiased juror, are to reach a wise decision, you need to be screened from inflammatory evidence adduced by a shrewd attorney, even an attorney you know to be biased.[6]

Summary of the Argument to this Point

We have argued that a person in self-deception is fruitfully and nonparadoxically thought of as both a deceiver and the deceived. There is no paradox because as deceiver our task is to construct a compelling story, not to decide whether it is true. We must also, though, decide whether the story is true. And because we are both attorney and juror, we know just how, as lawyer, we prepared the case. Although this knowledge seems to be enough to prevent us from being taken in by a weak case, it isn't. We may know that we ought to be skeptical, but not how skeptical.

We have argued, then, that 'self-deception' involves believing something you are motivated to believe. But we have argued that the motivation works indirectly, specifically by getting you to make a biased case for the belief you wish to have. The motivation does *not* lead directly to the having of some belief.

We have so far been regrettably general about the defense attorney's tricks—that is, how we convince ourselves about something and especially convince ourselves that we really haven't much tampered with the evidence. We look at these matters, now, in more detail.

How to Deceive Yourself by Underdiscounting

One reason you may underestimate just how much the data have been tampered with is that your reflection on the problem may reveal long stretches of honest examination. You may recall these moments when you worry that you are being excessively biased. We might call this the machine election model of self-deception. Consider the behavior of an old-fashioned political machine during an election. If the party appears to be doing very well, then there is no need for vote tampering and the vote will be untouched, fair, as any observer would report. On the other hand, if the vote in a particular district is just not as large as it needs to be and the election threatens to go astray, then resources (such as the population of drunk tanks and cemeteries) will be mobilized. (This way of handling election data was once traditional in Chicago and El Salvador.) But when the boss of such a machine writes his memoirs, he has no trouble honestly listing honest elections. By emphasizing this list he can paint a pleasing portrait wholly of genuine pigments. By directing his attention to the honest votes he reported, and away from the fact that they were honest only because there was no need for them to be otherwise, he convinces himself of his honesty.[7]

Slippery Slopes

There is another way that evidence of the importance of our cooking can become less and less salient, almost to the point of vanishing. We sometimes ignore first one, then another sign of our own bias—signs that are not particularly compelling taken one at a time—and find ourselves having missed something important, the degree to which we have become advocates rather than impartial assessors.

Consider this analogy. A person suffering a pain in her foot may well learn to avoid the pain by walking in a peculiar way. But this often happens so gradually that when someone points out the odd posture, the victim is genuinely surprised. She was aware of the original pain, and of her occasional attempts to avoid it, but not of the cumulative distortion her response to the pain produced. When the doctor mentions to her that her posture is lopsided, she may be genuinely surprised. She has slid down a postural slippery slope.

The father may have established habits of disattention and bland reinterpretation to early signs of rather minor trouble. He may have come to extend this disattention step by step to the gradually more serious signs of his daughter's dissolution. Although he intends each step—each minor cooking—he does not intend to go the distance his steps have added up to. He is sincerely surprised to discover how far he has gone. (This, of course, is the subject matter of the psychology of entrapment; see Sabini & Silver, 1982, chap. 4.)[8]

The Role of Unmotivated Cognitive Biases

There is substantial evidence that people are subject to general, unmotivated, innocent, cognitive biases, and these biases may *rein-*

force our motivated misinterpretations. It has been demonstrated, for instance (see Fischoff & Beyeth-Nelson, 1983, for a review) that subjects given a hypothesis to think about tend to look only for confirming cases, not disconfirming cases. This is innocent, unmotivated; people do this for a hypothesis they do not favor as well as for one they favor. Still, this bias can work tacitly to strengthen their belief even in data that they realize they have cooked.

The father may decide to entertain a less likely hypothesis than the one he wishes to avoid. Merely by framing and entertaining an alternative, the father is subject to confirmation bias and will tend to search for confirming rather than disconfirming evidence. He chooses to consider the hypothesis that long sleeves in the summer are stylish and not pursue the more likely hypothesis that his daughter wants to conceal something about her arms. He can also frame other self-serving hypotheses as the need arises. But once he does so, his natural tendency to be more sensitive to confirming evidence will make whatever hypothesis he picked look better than it should. And this makes it easier to neglect the special efforts that went into framing the hypothesis in the first place.

Mood and Distortion

There is by now a small literature on the effect of mood on cognition: being in a good (or bad) mood affects the way we think about things. For one thing, people in good moods seem to focus on the possible advantages of a course of action, and more or less ignore the possible disasters that may ensue. (See Isen, Means, Patrick, & Nowicki, 1982, on moods and the evaluation of evidence, and Clark & Fiske, 1982, on moods and cognition in general.) Someone in a good or bad mood is searching the world in a biased way, but he needn't know it—indeed, typically doesn't know it. Thus, this bias alone isn't self-deception. But this sort of passive, innocent bias may also play a role in self-deception. Let us return to the father with the possibly addicted daughter.

He sees something that causes the hypothesis that she is a drug addict to enter his mind. That is a painful thought and he knows it; he doesn't want to think it again, and he knows that. He thinks instead of an alternative possibility, perhaps an unlikely one, but one that can explain his observation. He considers this hypothesis. Perhaps he realizes that he is biased. But because he is prey to confirmation bias, and because thinking this alternative puts him in a better mood and makes him more sanguine about this happier alternative, he becomes more biased than he started out. And he doesn't know this. Because he knows he has become biased, he may discount his belief in this new hypothesis. But he is unlikely to discount enough. So, given the availability of cognitive bias, self-deception becomes not a neat and rather difficult trick but something it is hard not to fall into. On our account we can even fool ourselves merely by not framing painful alternatives. This is an easy failing, indeed.

UNCONSCIOUS PROCESSING AND SELF-DECEPTION

There is a long tradition in psychology of seeing self-deception as really a matter of unconscious processing of information. One line of research in this tradition attempted to show, for example, that words that had been previously paired with shock were less readily recognized than were neutral words; yet the subjects made physiological responses to these words (Lazarus & McCleary, 1951). This evidence suggested that the subjects unconsciously recognized the words, since how else could they have a physiological response to them? And, indeed, the evidence suggested that something about the history of the words' being paired with shock prevented the words' meaning from coming into consciousness. (See Erdely,

1974, for a more recent study of this sort.) Robert Zajonc (1980) is the most recent champion of this research tradition. He claims to have shown that subjects can come to form preferences for stimuli without recognizing them.

We have not discussed this work here, for two reasons. First, as long as this tradition is, there is an equally long tradition of criticism of the work on methodological and other grounds. (See Mandler, 1984, and Parrott & Sabini, 1989, for recent criticisms.) Second, and more important, unconscious processing of information is a red herring in a discussion of self-deception.

We have argued that a person fully conscious of all that he does can deceive himself. So the unconscious processing of information isn't necessary to self-deception. Further, just because a person unconsciously processes information doesn't mean that he is in self-deception. The processing of information about syntactic category boundaries in the parsing of a sentence is unconscious, but it would hardly do to claim that all understandings of sentences are, therefore, examples of self-deception. For the unconscious processing of information to be self-deception it must meet exactly the same criteria that the conscious processing of information must meet to constitute self-deception. This is why unconscious processing is a red herring.

But even if unconscious processing of information is neither necessary to nor sufficient for self-deception, it might be a common way to deceive ourselves. But, for all the ink that psychologists have devoted to ideas like 'subliminal perception,' there has been little attention to the question of how large a role such things actually play. We suspect (but only suspect) that they play a very small part. Indeed, we suspect that the reason psychologists believe that unconscious processing is key was not that they discovered that unconscious processing played a prominent role, but that they believed that unconscious processing was conceptually required. Once we abandon this belief, we can probably dispense with unconscious processing as a constituent of self-deception altogether.

Is Self-Deception Always Wrong?

David Hamlyn (1971) has raised a question that we would like to touch on: What is the moral status of self-deception? For Kant, lying is always wrong, thus self-deception is always wrong. But what can we say to those who do not condemn telling white lies or intentionally misdirecting would-be killers? Is there still something wrong, morally, with self-deception? Is there anything wrong with deceiving yourself other than that it is a deception?

We think not. It is true enough that a person may, by deceiving himself, come to do some other evil; by stilling his conscience with a pleasant lie, he liberates himself to do wrong. But in this case one condemns the evil, not the lie. Or, perhaps one condemns the lie by virtue of its being a means to an evil end.[9] But what about cases where pleasant lies lead to no evil? What is their moral status?

A mother refuses to believe that her son has died in the war despite very good evidence. She might do this for several reasons. Perhaps she does it to keep herself in readiness for his return—just in case. This isn't self-deception. But perhaps she does it because she finds the belief in her son's death too painful to face. Is her self-deception immoral?

Of course, her behavior could easily lead to immoral, or pragmatically regrettable, consequences. Perhaps by deceiving herself that her son is still alive she does not carry out the terms of his will, something he would have wanted. But, then again, the only effect of her deceiving herself might be that she lives out the remainder of her life without the pain of knowing that her son was killed. Is this *immoral*?

We think not. Still, her refusal to face painful facts is a defect.

The natural thing to say of her, we suggest, is that she lacks courage. But being a coward isn't evil, and it doesn't necessarily lead to evil, but it is, necessarily, a weakness, a *flaw of character*. And, as we have argued elsewhere (see chapter 2), flaws of character, such as cowardice, are rather different from immorality.[10] Thus, along with Hamlyn (1971), and contra Champlain (1977) and Lineham (1982), we believe that self-deception is *not* intrinsically *evil*, but we do claim that it does, intrinsically, express a flaw of character.

Conclusion

The concept of "self-deception" is not paradoxical. Nor does it refer to deceit or error. A person who is fooling herself is both the victimizer intentionally deceiving herself and the victim who has been deceived. She knows that deception has occurred, since she has done it, but cannot gauge its extent—so she is deceived. In order for a person to be said to be fooling herself she must know, or at one time have known, that she was cooking data because of the way the evidence made her feel—although her realization is necessarily partial. If a person is not aware at any point that she is handling some of the data improperly, then she may be biased but she is not deceiving herself.

The self-deceiver is attempting to manipulate her own psychological state, not the state of the world. This is what distinguishes the person who has deceived herself from the hypocrite. The hypocrite, whether she convinces herself by cooked data or is just feigning, is presenting her state of mind in order to get something from the world—typically esteem, a reputation for virtue.

The self-deceiver is not necessarily doing anything morally wrong—assuming that lying isn't necessarily wrong—but she shows herself to be unable or unwilling to face the world. Her flaw is cowardice; she is necessarily shamed but not necessarily guilty (see chapter 6).

Notes

This chapter was written with Maria Miceli of the Instituto di Psicologia, Consiglio Nazionale della Ricerche, Rome, Italy.

1. The complementary view of self-deception as a peculiar form of deceit—as opposed to error—may be extracted from Goffman's work, especially *The Presentation of Self in Everyday Life* (1959). For Goffman, the deceptions, and self-deceptions, required to maintain our self-presentations are typically so frequent, practiced, and habitual that they are beneath our notice. It's not that we could not spell out the inconsistency in our performance if asked, but rather that we rarely bother; we deceive and are consequently self-deceived absentmindedly. The Freudian view is also one of self-deception as really a form of deceit—a case of deliberate deception of the self by an unconscious fragment of the self (see Fingarette, 1982, for a discussion).

The contributors to Jon Elster's *The multiple self* (1986) clarify the various senses in which a self might be thought of as divided, and how such divisions might play a role in explaining self-deception. Divided selves are repaired to because unitary selves do not seem to be the sort of thing that can fool and be fooled. In this chapter we shall attempt to demonstrate that unitary selves can manage this feat.

2. Further, these feelings are often more malleable than the reality. Emotions are at hand to manipulate, while the realization of the desired states in the world may be far off. This is one reason to prefer the immediate emotion to the more distant reality. And insofar as someone succumbs for this reason, his flaw may be seen as an instance of 'weakness of the will' (See Szavabados, 1985, on the relations between 'self-deception' and 'weakness of the will'.)

3. It is easier to make this distinction than to apply it. This is so in part because motives are notoriously susceptible to reframing. Still, we claim two things. First, if, and only if, we were to find that a person's motive was to manipulate her psychological state would we call her deceiving herself. And second, we believe there is a fact of the matter, that motives may be slippery, but they aren't imaginary. Therefore,

though the ascription of motives to people may be treacherous, it isn't whimsical, groundless. We may not often (or for that matter ever) be incorrigibly certain in our ascriptions, but we can have good (or bad) reasons for them.

4. Of course, amassing evidence and judging the person on the basis of the evidence cannot be as facilely separated as this metaphor suggests. We shall articulate some of the ways they intrude on one another. And the ways they intrude on each other make self-deception all the easier to pull off. What we want to stress here is that even *without* these complexities self-deception is empirically possible and conceptually coherent. If self-deception is possible in a world in which evidence and judgment are as different as the positivists would have it, it is surely possible in a world in which they are as intertwined as Kuhn and Quine would have it.

5. So, self-deception does not require total ignorance, although many students of matter have thought that it does. For instance, Fingarette (1969) holds that a person in self-deception must not only refrain from "spelling out" the details of a commitment but also must also have a policy not to spell out that she is doing so.

6. Our court metaphor might be altered in one respect. A court is supposed to be concerned with establishing the truth—guilt or innocence. If our thesis is correct, the person who deceives himself is less concerned with establishing or falsifying facts, per se, then he is with procuring a psychological state—the state that these "facts" would entail. For instance, the father's self-deception about his daughter's addition is not so much an attempt to compel reality, or even an attempt to rig his daughter's innocence, as an attempt to avoid being upset about the issue. This involves a belief in his daughter's innocence as an intermediate goal, but since his ultimate goal is avoidance of upset, he will be lenient about what passes for acceptable evidence. Imagine one of Daumier's judges whose main interest in disposing of a case is in how soon he can get to lunch and one decision will get the mess over with quicker than the other.

7. A related trick involves juggling measures, standards, and indicators that are allowable gauges of what we wish to measure, but always selecting the one that will give us the best result at the moment. When one measure falters, others may temporarily give more pleasing results. We know that we are cooking, "prejudiced," but since we are

honorably using the measures we should use, we tend to underdiscount our tampering. Indeed, deceit, ignorance, and self-deception may sometimes by symbiotic. The father may have to invent excuses for his daughter's odd behavior in front of relatives, and he may be completely aware that he is doing so; yet he may have fooled himself into believing that there is nothing really wrong with her and that his excuses, or deceits, are just for convenience. Further, there are things that the daughter must be careful to conceal from daddy. She must help his self-deception along. If her "works" were found, then the evidence would be too blatant for her father to ignore. Goffman (1959) suggests that in order to inhabit our roles successfully, we often must swing from cynical manipulation of others to self-deception to sincerity and back again.

8. Sometimes people don't gradually step up their disattentions, but rather an initial failure may be all that is necessary to cause the person not to be able to discover the truth in the future. In this case, although we might say that the ignorance resulted from an act of self-deception, we would not say the person was deceiving himself. Indeed, he may be trying to discover the truth with all his wits, yet not be able to undo his initial act. Szavabados (1985) argues that we usually reserve the phrase "wishful thinking" for simple isolated acts of motivated belief in the absence or against the evidence, and that only when there is a pattern of intentional misapprehension of the evidence do we say that a person is deceiving herself.

9. But isn't it just wrong to ignore evidence that is before our eyes? We can't and shouldn't follow up on all of our suspicions. Some things are none of our business. Let us suppose that we do not follow up on one of these nosey suspicions, and come to misappraise the situation on that account. Would we say that we had deceived ourselves? No. We are 'guilty' of not following up on a suspicion only if it's the sort of suspicion that one should follow up on. The "should" here could be pragmatic or aesthetic as well as moral.

10. To summarize our argument, cowardice is not a moral flaw because (1) we would call a person a coward even if we believed that she could not help it, but we don't (morally) blame people for what they can't help; (2) the concept of transgression implies obligations transgressed against. Did the mother have an obligation to believe that her son was dead? Except, perhaps, for a Kantian, no. For this reason,

we would argue that the pain we feel on discovering that we have been deceiving ourselves is that of humiliation (or shame) and not guilt (see chapter 6 on this distinction).

References

Canfield, J., & Gustavson, D. (1962). Self-deception. *Analysis, 23,* 32–36.

Champlain, T. S. (1977). Self-deception—A reflexive dilemma. *Philosophy, 52,* 281–299.

Clark, M. S., & Fiske, S. T. (Eds.) (1982). *Affect and cognition: The 17th annual Carnegie symposium on cognition.* Hillsdale, N.J.: Erlbaum.

Elster, J. (Ed.) (1986). *The multiple self.* New York: Cambridge University Press.

Erdelyi, M. H. (1974). A new look at the new look: Perceptual defense and vigilance. *Psychological Review, 81,* 1–25.

Fingarette, H. (1969). *Self-deception.* London: Routledge and Kegan Paul.

Fingarette, H. (1982). Self-deception and the 'splitting of the ego'. In R. Wollheim and J. Hopkins (Eds.), *Philosophical essays on Freud* (pp. 212–228). Cambridge: Cambridge University Press.

Fischoff, B., & Beyeth-Nelson, R. (1983). Hypothesis evaluation from a Bayesian perspective. *Psychological Review, 90,* 139–260.

Gardner, P. (1969–70). Error, faith and self-deception. *Proceedings of the Aristotelian Society, 70,* 221–243.

Goffman, E. (1959). *The presentation of self in everyday life.* Garden City, N.Y.: Anchor.

Hamlyn, D. W. (1971). Self-deception. *Proceedings of the Aristotelian Society, 45,* 45–60.

Isen, A. M., Means, B., Patrick, R., & Nowicki, G. (1982). Some factors influencing decision-making strategy and risk taking. In M. S. Clark & S. T. Fiske (Eds.), *Affect and cognition: The 17th annual Carnegie symposium on cognition* (pp. 243–261). Hillsdale, N.J.: Erlbaum.

Lazarus, R. S., & McCleary, R. A. (1951). Autonomic discrimination without awareness: A study of subception. *Psychological Review, 58,* 113–122.

Lineham, E. (1982). Ignorance, self-deception and moral accountability. *Journal of Value Inquiry, 16,* 101–115.

Mandler, G. (1984). *Mind and body: Psychology of emotion and stress.* New York: Norton.

Parrott, W. G., & Sabini, J. (1989). On the "emotional" qualities of certain types of cognition: A reply to argument for the independence of cognition and affect. *Cognitive Therapy and Research, 13,* 49–65.

Ross, L., Lepper, M. R., & Hubbard, M. (1975). Perseverance in self-perception and social perception: Biased attributional processes in the debriefing paradigm. *Journal of Personality and Social Psychology, 32,* 880–892.

Sabini, J., & Silver, M. (1982). *Moralities of everyday life.* New York: Oxford University Press.

Sabini, J., & Silver, M. (1998). Loyalty. Manuscript.

Sartre, J. P. (1943/1982). *Mauvaise foi* and the unconscious. In R. Wollheim and J. Hopkins (Eds.), *Philosophical essays on Freud* (pp. 203–212). Cambridge: Cambridge University Press.

Silver, M., Conte, R., Miceli, M., & Poggi, I. (1986). Humiliation: Feeling, social control, and the construction of identity. *Journal for the Theory of Social Behaviour, 16,* 269–285.

Szavbados, B. (1985). The self, its passions and self-deceptions. In M. Martin (Ed.), *Self-deception and self understanding: New essays in philosophy and psychology.* Lawrence: Kansas University.

Zajonc, R. B. (1980). Feeling and thinking: Preferences need no inferences. *American Psychologist, 35,* 151–175.

8

On the Possible Nonexistence of Emotions

The Passions

In this chapter we want to ask whether there is a unique psychology of the emotions. That is, we want to know whether there are phenomena of our mental lives that are uniquely the province of the emotions or whether emotional phenomena are also something else. Since no one would raise this question who planned to answer it (unprovocatively) yes, there is no point in our not coming clean and letting on that we plan to answer no—at least in regard to a subset of the emotions. We want to argue in this chapter that belief and desire psychology is an adequate psychology; it does not leave something out—emotions.

We shall defend the narrow claim that the subset of the emotions that may be thought of was the passions doesn't exist; that is, we shall claim that there are no elements of the mental economy corresponding to the emotions of anger, envy, jealousy, fear, and maybe a few others.[1] A test for whether something belongs in the category of the passions is whether a person can be said both to be x (or feel x) and act out of x (where by 'act' one means engage in goal-directed action—i.e., act on a motive).

Anyone who wants to argue what we argue must bear a heavy burden: commonsense thought and talk suppose that we have emotional lives, and that the emotional lives we have are important. So, claiming what we claim, we had better be prepared to explain how it is possible for people to think and talk about emotion in the way they do even though there are no such things as emotions. In the first part of this chapter, that is just what we shall do. We shall argue that people do indeed have experiences, feelings, that lead them to talk about their emotions, and that this talk isn't pointless, fatuous, or metaphysical. But it also doesn't imply that there are elements of our mental lives called emotions that are somehow in addition to our beliefs and desires.[2] Then we shall show how our position relates to some historically important theories of emotion (Dewey, 1895; James, 1890/1950; Peters, 1972; Schachter & Singer, 1962) and to some current theories (Buck, 1985; Ekman, 1973; Ekman & Davidson, 1994; Frijda, Kuipers, & ter Schure, 1989; Frank, 1988; Lazarus, 1991; Roseman, Wiest & Swartz, 1994). Finally, we shall draw out some of the implications of our view.

EMOTIONS IN COMMONSENSE PSYCHOLOGY

Our thinking about this question begins by trying to imagine what human experience would be like absent the emotions. Fortunately, we do not have to start that exercise from scratch. Surely you remember *Star Trek* and the Vulcans? They are uncomfortably alien: they have no emotions. But in other ways, perhaps all other ways, they are just like us. Because of this, thinking about the Vulcans is a tool for thinking about the notion of emotion and why it is important.

At first blush it might seem that creatures who lack emotion must lack certain sorts of *desires* that we humans have—not all the desires we have, they get hungry. But it might seem that lacking emotions they *must* lack *certain* motives, like, say, loyalty—motives that are often thought of as having close connections to feelings. But, as it happens, this isn't so. The Vulcans are portrayed, at least, as being among the most loyal members of the Federation, and this portrayal doesn't jolt our sensibilities. So lacking emotions doesn't seem to constrain, at least in any obvious way, the kinds of motives a creature can have.[3] Yet they are felt to be alien. But why? What is the difference between having desires (which Vulcans do) and having emotions as well (which Vulcans don't)?

But, of course, these questions presuppose something. They presuppose that emotions and motives are things, different things. They presuppose that one could, by exploring the mental life of a human (but not a Vulcan), find something that is the emotion in the case of the human, but not in the case of the Vulcan. Exactly how one explores the mental lives of Vulcans and humans will vary depending on the kind of psychologist you are; you might probe with functional MRI, or reaction times, or EMG of facial expressions, or even introspect, but however you do it you will expect to find emotions in the mental life of the human but not the Vulcan. And you will expect to find motives there in both cases.

The issue of whether emotions and motives are separate entities or not may at first appear esoteric, or at least without any theoretical consequences—sometimes it seems that way even to us. But some important issues hang on the answer to this question. It would seem important to those who want to make arguments about how and why the emotions evolved (e.g., Frank, 1988), how and why the emotions are expressed (Ekman, 1973), and how emotions function in the mental economy (e.g., Lazarus, 1991) to know whether there is a there there.

Emotions and Desires Intertwined

To bring our discussion of the relation of emotion to desire to earth, we need a place where we can find lots of emotion, irrationality, willfulness, and even a few motives, disguised and undisguised: a faculty meeting. Imagine an assistant professor listening to a fatuous senior colleague. Imagine there welling up in this untenured person a desire to make a cutting remark. But, let us further imagine, our assistant professor considers his position carefully and decides that it is in his best interest to let the remarks go rather than to give in to his anger. Of course, like any soap opera there are many intelligible ways this plot can work itself out. The question we want to answer is: Which of the stories depicts emotions (as Captain Kirk, a human on the *Enterprise*, has them) and which could just as well have been told about a Vulcan faculty meeting?

In one continuation, the poor fellow—*despite* his decision—gives in to his anger and lashes out. Here is a case where we are very likely to speak of someone being emotional, carried away with emotion, letting his emotions get the better of him. This is a human, not a Vulcan story. Now imagine instead that the outburst isn't from an assistant professor, but is from a senior person who feels the same strong desire to lash out, realizes that she has nothing to lose, and so decides to speak out. Imagine her lashing out at the appropriate moment. Here again we have action motivated by anger to be sure, but this action is less likely to be described in emotion terms.

We follow Peters (1972) in claiming that the same word can be used to pick out either a motive or an emotion. So anger, for example, can be used to explain why someone did something (unemotionally) or to describe the emotional state someone is in. Like Peters, we are interested in when 'anger', say, is used to indicate the motive someone has in acting versus when it is used to indicate emotional state. We claim that both of our protagonists were motivated by anger, but only the junior person was overcome by emotion.

The reason we are less likely to speak of emotion in the senior person's case is that her lashing out was the *product of a decision* and not something *flying in the face of a decision*. The point is that, in asserting that someone is emotional or acting out of an emotion, we are claiming that his action is not the sort that would result from a proper consideration of the consequences and that he knows or, perhaps, should know this. So there are contextual details that make the assistant professor's lashing out a strictly human emotion, but the senior professor's as likely to happen on Vulcan as it is on earth. And this is true even though the mental and physiological contents (including arousal) in both cases *are identical*. It is entirely plausible that both folks are saying to themselves nothing more than "I am finally going to shut that fatuous fool up."

Who Is to Say What Is Unwise: A Digression

On the view we are developing, then, emotions are invoked when behavior is in the service of some understandable motive—the desire to quiet the annoying is surely something we all understand but is unwise.[4] This inevitably leads to the question: Unwise in whose eyes? Well, to a first approximation it is unwise in the eyes of whoever is calling the action emotional. So, to call an action emotional is to claim that it was sensible but unwise, and this is true whether the actor herself is characterizing her state or an observer is. But suppose actor and observer disagree; suppose the (paternal) department chair chides the junior fellow for his emotional quip, pointing out that it isn't always the best idea to insult one's senior colleagues (grateful though he surely would be for the quip), but the fellow denies that he was emotional, that emotion played any role. Who is right? How would we decide?

Different cases demand different answers. Imagine that the junior person goes on to say, "Oh my God, I hadn't realized that!" Now anyone who believes him, that it hadn't occurred to him that he was causing himself trouble, will believe that he was stupid or thoughtless, but not that he was in the grips of emotion. Of course, if he is chronically obtuse about such things, the listener will be more secure in this conclusion.

Suppose he replies to the chair that though he no doubt won the enmity of that particular senior colleague, surely he won the gratitude of many more. Now suppose that on reflection the chair agrees. Surely he would no longer believe his junior colleague had been emotional and he would withdraw his claim since our assistant professor had pointed to an adequate justification for his behavior.[5] In all of these cases the person with the more compelling facts about whether the action followed from a broad consideration of goals, values, strategies, abilities, and so on is the one who is better able to make a case for the presence or absence of emotion.

Emotional experience is much more common than are full-blown examples of imprudence—even at faculty meetings. Let us see how our assistant professor might have an emotional experience without jeopardizing tenure.

Emotions That Aren't Public

Imagine that he does not lash out but that as he tries to concentrate on the fascinating details of the latest attempt at curriculum reform, he finds his heart racing, his fists forming, and his mind turning to cutting remarks he wishes he could make. And imagine that he cannot, or can only with difficulty, inhibit these happenings. He is in the grip of emotion even if he behaves like Spock and is discrete for the rest of the meeting.

The important thing to note about these emotional experiences is that, although there is no acting out of the motive of anger, the elements of the experience of (the emotion of) anger—the pounding heart, the clenched fists, and especially the mental rehearsal of cutting remarks—might be described as preparing to act out of anger. Indeed, the only reason *not* to see the reactions the assistant professor is having as preparations for action is that he will not in fact act on them, and he knows that. The rehearsal of the cutting remarks would be a genuine preparation were it not for the fact that he has already (wisely) decided that the performance the rehearsals are preparations for will never be given. So in this (common) case of emotion there is no action worth speaking of, but there is a body and a mind preparing itself to serve the desire for action. And it is just these preparations that are the evidence for the claim that the person is experiencing an emotion; they are the stuff of the emotional experience. But they are also the manifestion of an aroused desire.

We have claimed that emotional experiences are often the experience of preparing for an action without acting, but we are not claiming that *all* fantasies are emotional. It isn't the fact that the junior fellow is fantasizing a crushing remark about his colleague's last paper—back in the Jurassic period—that tips us (and him) off that he is emotional, but rather it is that he *cannot help but* fantasize this, even when he tries to concentrate on something else. This is what never happens to Vulcans. It's not that they don't make remarks about the Jurassic papers of their colleagues; rather, it is that if they decide not to mention such things, they can stop thinking about them.

We sometimes (even usually) are able to suppress motives in the sense that we decide not to act on them and succeed in not acting. Still, we may not entirely suppress them; the motivational states remain alive in us, commanding our attention, our cognitive resources, and our physiological states. We can, within limits, decide not to do what we really want to, but we cannot simply decide to ignore, to not be bothered by, some desires.

Summary

So we have two ways, then, that humans are different from Vulcans. We are different from them in that we sometimes do things that we know that we shouldn't because we are overwhelmed by desire. And we sometimes find ourselves devoting cognitive and other resources to preparations to act even though we are quite certain we will not act and we would prefer not to act. A Vulcan would decide what is best and act on it, without turning back.[6]

TRADITIONAL THEORIES IN CONTRAST TO THE NO-EMOTION VIEW

In our view, one talks about emotions when motives (or desires) of a certain sort are experienced but not acted on, or when they are acted on despite a decision not to. We believe, then, that people talk about emotions only when there is a conflict, a conflict among motives or between a motive and a decision. John Dewey (1895) was there first. According to his theory, emotional experiences are produced by conflict, conflict among motives or perhaps between motives and other things—decisions, for instance—or even the conflict inherent in the inhibition and delay of tendencies that are necessary for a coordinated response. But Dewey (in contrast to us) had a realist theory of the emotions: conflict gives rise to certain sorts of experiences and these experiences are emotions. In our position, on the other hand, circumstances trigger desires, *motivational* states. These desires include or produce certain sorts of experiences (physiologies, for that matter). If these experiences are had in the right circumstances, they will be seen as emotional. On our view, in contrast to Dewey's, there are no experiences that are uniquely emotional; rather, the experiences of emotion are also the experiences of desire (or motivation).

To put the same point a bit differently, we share with Dewey an emphasis on conflict as the source of emotion, but we differ from him in this way: Dewey does not ask whether (or doubt that) emotion and desire (motivation) are distinct mental entities; he assumes they are. He sees the relationship between conflict and emotion as *causal*. We do raise the question of the independent existence of emotion and motivation and see the relation between conflict and emotion in a different way. We see emotional experience as essentially the experience of desire, but we believe that *in the proper context* some experiences of desires are called experiences of emotion.

James on Emotion

William James, too, had a theory of emotion. Well, maybe it would be fair to say he had several theories of emotion. He had that famous one about how the perception of a bodily state *is* the emotion. But he also talked about the relation of emotions to 'instincts'—which for our purposes might as well be motives or desires. Let us see what he had to say about that.

> In speaking of the instincts it has been impossible to keep them separate from the emotional excitements which go with them. Objects of rage, love, fear, etc., not only prompt a man to outward deeds, but provoke characteristic alterations in his attitude and visage, and affect his breathing, circulation, and other organic functions in specific ways. When the outward deeds are inhibited, these latter emotional expressions still remain, and we read the anger in the face, though the blow may not be struck, and the fear betrays itself in voice and color, though one may suppress all other signs. *Instinctive reactions and emotional expressions thus shade imperceptibly into each other. Every object that excites an instinct excites an emotion as well.* Emotions, however, fall short of

instincts in that the emotional reaction usually terminates in the subject's own body whilst the instinctive reaction is apt to go further and enter into practical relations with the exciting object. (1890/1950, p. 442; emphasis, of course, in original)

If you accept James's 'instinct' for our 'motivation', then like us James comes close to eliminating emotional states as distinct from motivational states.[7]

If you take our view or Dewey's, or even James's, one thing you must deny is that being in a particular emotional state *causes* a motivational state. None of us accords the emotions this sort of causal priority over motivation. This means, of course, that none of us will describe an encounter with a bear as one in which you see the bear, experience the emotion of fear, and then run because of the emotion. We all want to describe it in some other way. James would say (famously) that you see the bear, run (and have some bodily reactions), which you then notice (at some point). It is the noticing of the reaction that *IS* the emotion for James. The emotion, then, certainly isn't the cause of the running. For Dewey, insofar as you just run unconflictedly, you will *not* experience the emotion of fear. We say this: you run, and you may or may not notice your state. If you do, you would be right to describe the state as fear, but you would have no reason to talk specifically of the emotion of fear unless you thought there was something untoward about your running—perhaps there was some reason you should *not* have run away.

Many people, the current authors included, have had the experience of running away from a danger, and some of us have reported that the fear sets in but not while running. As Dewey recounts, "I remember well a youthful fight with the emotions of irritation and anger before and of partial fear and partial pride afterwards, but as to the intervening period of the fight nothing but a strangely vivid perception of the other boy's face as the hypnotizing focus of all muscular activities" (p. 29). Dewey would argue that there is no experience of the emotion of fear in these examples because there is no conflict. One merely flees the bear or fights one's enemy. For James the experience of fear may *not* necessarily occur—that is, it is possible that you will happen not to introspect on your running. Presumably while you are fleeing the bear you may be too busy to introspect.

We would suggest that to call running away an emotional reaction is to suggest that bears are not the sort of thing it is wise to flee. Now running away from a domestic cat or a parakeet—that's a sign of emotion; in those cases we would call what we see emotion precisely because domestic cats and parakeets aren't threats. Fleeing what isn't a threat is against one's better judgment and, hence, a sign of emotion.

CONTEMPORARY THEORIES OF EMOTION

Before we discuss contemporary psychological theories of the emotions we should touch on the philosophical account closest to ours, that of R. S. Peters. For Peters (1972), that which differentiates, say, a motive or emotion of anger from one of fear that each has a distinctive appraisal; anger involves the appraisal that one has been insulted, fear that one is in danger. What differentiates the motive of fear from the emotion of fear is that in the former the appraisal provides reason for doing something—we act out of fear; in the latter, the appraisal leads to a set of "passive" phenomena that come over one upon making the appraisal—disturbances of judgment. Peters denies that emotions or motives pick out "distinctive items in the furniture of the mind"; rather, when we point to passive phenomena issuing from a "mental act of appraisal," we speak of emotions; when we are interested in actions flowing from the mental act of appraisal, we speak of motives.

Clearly there are close affinities between Peters's theory and our own. But there are differences, too. On Peters's account, there is a reason the motive of anger and the emotion of anger share the name 'anger': they share an appraisal—the motive and the emotion both follow from the same appraisal of an insult. For us, though, their relation is tighter than that. The emotion *IS* the motive in a particular context. It is not a surprise in our account that anger the motive and anger the emotion should share the same name, since the latter is just the former under trying circumstances. Many of what Peters calls passive phenomena are, for us, simply signs of aroused motivation. True, these passive manifestations are likely to be *more common* in the case of inhibited action, emotion, than when action is uninhibited—as James pointed out (see above), and also true that they may be the only manifestations of the desire in cases of inhibition (also as James pointed out). Because both these things are true, the presence of the passive manifestations is likely to be a symptom of emotion, but the symptoms aren't criterial. You can have emotions without them, and symptoms without emotion.

SCHACHTER AND SINGER

Schachter and Singer (1962) are widely believed to have proposed a theory of emotion.[8] And they certainly conducted a very famous experiment. We now ask if Schachter and Singer have a general theory of emotion, how does it relate to ours and what does it have to say about the relation of motivation to emotion? And then we ask, their theory aside, how do their *data* relate to our theory?

Like James, they believe that if one were to strip away from an emotional experience the internal arousal, then one would be left with something too pallid to be called an emotion. So for James, and for Schachter and Singer, the crucial "felt" element of an emotion is physiological arousal. But Schachter and Singer add an additional element. They argue that an emotional experience isn't just the experience of physiological arousal; added to that is a cognitive element, a belief about what caused that arousal. So for them, anger is, say, the experience of physiological arousal interpreted as having been caused by an insult (or, perhaps, frustration). Where, one might ask, is motivation in all of this? What happened to James's instincts that reach out for commerce with the world into which the emotions imperceptibly blend? What happened to James's pragmatism?

Well, at least two things happened: decades of frowning by psychologists on the notion of an instinct, and a decade or so of Hullian psychology with its emphasis on generalized drive states. It isn't that Schachter and Singer, in their theorizing about emotion, dismiss motives, desires, or instincts as irrelevant. Not at all. It's rather that these concepts don't figure in their discussion.[9] Let us be explicit about Schachter and Singer's theory about a particular emotional episode, so we can ask about the relation of motivation and emotion, even though they don't discuss it.

Consider our assistant professor again. He hears that "bear" of a full professor spout off again. He appraises himself as insulted and demeaned by being exposed to this stuff again. Many things happen in the wake of his feeling that way—recall that we left him with clenched fists, a racing heart, and a consciousness filled with plans for revenge. But among these elements are signs of generalized, physiological arousal—the pounding heart. As Schachter and Singer might tell the story, he then notices his physiological arousal and asks himself: why am I aroused? (He unconsciously asks himself this question, of course.) He decides it was because of the insult. Once he has reached that conclusion (and *only* once he has reached that conclusion) he is, according to Schachter and Singer, angry. This theory seems to be a day late and a dollar short with the anger (at least in the sense of a motivational state).

It seems more natural to say that our assistant professor was angry before he noticed anything at all about his mental state. And, indeed, it seems natural to think that his noticing these elements of his mental state was *how he knew* he was angry, not *how he became* angry. After all, suppose he did lash out and attack his colleague and was so focused on that (like Dewey on his opponent's face) that he was too busy to be hypothesizing about the source of his arousal. Does that mean he was too busy to *be* angry? Or does it mean he was too busy to *notice* he was angry? (Schachter, of course, inherited this problem from James.) The motivational state of anger, wanting to lash out, doesn't seem to need to wait for self-reflection.

Then, if our angry young man should ask himself—for some reason—what state is he in? Why isn't he allowed to notice that he is plotting revenge or action in the world? Why is he stuck with noticing only generalized arousal and an analysis of its possible cause? If we allow him to notice his very focused desire to make devastating remarks, is it at all plausible that he will need to hypothesize about causes of arousal to decide what state he is in? Of course, for Schachter and Singer's theory, generalized arousal is useful since it is common to love, hate, anger, jealousy, joy, and so on. But what about the Schachter and Singer experiment? How do their *data* bear on our theory?

To give them every benefit of statistical doubt, they found that if a subject is insulted (or placed in a room with a pile of junk and a confederate who wants to have some fun with it), then the subject will act in an angry (euphoric) way and they will report themselves as being angry (euphoric). Moreover, they will report and express more of these emotions if they have been injected with adrenaline. However, if they are told that the injection produces generalized arousal as a side effect, then they do not become emotional or report emotion.

Much, then, of what Schachter and Singer found is that adrenaline intensifies emotional experience. And surely this is not a problem for any theory—it no doubt increases motivation as well. Perhaps in addition to this Schachter and Singer might have wanted their results to show that if arousal is produced *without* a justifying context, then subjects will, nonetheless, try to find an adequate source and label (and experience) their emotion accordingly. Unfortunately, their experiment was singularly unsuited to *that* task. The subjects in the anger condition, for example, were asked questions like: Which member of your immediate family bathes less than once a week? How many extramarital affairs has your mother had? These would seem to be perfectly adequate stimuli to provoke anger.

The curious finding in the Schachter and Singer experiment, then, is that when people are told they have been given a drug that produces physiological arousal, they report (and express) very little emotion, even less than the placebo group given no adrenaline. On the face of it, this seems to be an embarrassment to *our* theory. After all, our theory claims that emotions are, at their heart, motivations, so imagine the parallel experiment with hunger. We find a drug that intensifies hunger, and we tell people it does that. Would we expect them, because they knew that drug caused their experience, *not* to report hunger? Would we expect them—because they are informed—not to eat? So why are Schachter and Singer's informed subjects so placid? Well, though in general they are less emotional than the placebo group, this difference is never significant (in four tries). And this finding has not been replicated (Marshall & Zimbardo, 1979; Maslach, 1979). So it might not be wise to dismiss our theory just because of this result. And even if it is true that people informed that their state was produced by a drug behave differently from those not so informed, this might tell us more about people's attitudes toward drugs than it does about their emotions.

Schachter and Singer, we suggest, have proposed a needlessly cumbersome theory, one that ignores the fact that people who are in emotional states want to do particular things. They aren't just experiencing arousal and wondering why; they are plotting revenge, or their escape from the trap they are in, or how to do in the competitor for their straying mate, and so on. These plans aren't the product of self-knowledge; they are the basis for self-knowledge.

Frank's Evolutionary Theory

Why did the emotions evolve? What selective advantage did having emotions confer? Are organisms better off with them than without them? Our view of the emotions has implicit in it answers to these questions. They didn't evolve. They don't confer selective advantage; *motives* evolved and *they,* presumably, confer selective advantage. We aren't better off with emotions than without them. In our view, the human phenomena that most clearly evoke the notion of emotion arise because we are, unlike the Vulcans, not wholly able to suppress (or fully suppress) our urges (motives). The emotions, in this view, are the best possible evidence for the evolution of the human mind—they show how it is imperfect.

Recently, however, some theorists have proposed that the emotions did evolve, do serve a purpose, and are good for us. One such prominent theorist is Frank (1988). It is illuminating to put his account besides ours.

Frank's theory can best be worked out by considering a story much like our assistant professor's story.[10] Imagine that a bully visits a schoolyard. He sees a smaller child and confiscates her bat. What would be rational for the smaller child to do—fight for her bat? She will then add the bruises of a losing fight to the loss of a bat. Rationally she should just let the bat go. Of course, the bully too can calculate what is rational for the little kid to do. Thus, he knows he can take the bat (and anything else he wants) with impunity. Frank argues, then, that rationality (at least in such circumstances) leaves us open to exploitation by bullies (cf. pp. x–xi, 1–19).

Now what if the child were constituted that such a theft would so upset her that she would fight the bully as hard and long as she could despite knowing that she could not win? Her outcome would be worse—more bruises and still no bat. *But* the bully might very well avoid her for easier prey next time. So though it might not be in her short-term best interest to fight the bully, it might be in her long-term best interest.

But now let us imagine that the bully is a visitor from Australia and will be returning there this afternoon—facts well known to the victim of the bat theft. Now what should she do—what is in her long-term interest? Well, considering this bully alone, it would certainly seem that it is in her interest to let the bat go; deterring him from future marauding is hardly in her interest, unless her family is discussing a move to Sydney in the near future. But suppose other bullies who live closer to home are witnesses to the interchange between the bully and the little girl. And suppose they are deterred. Now, again, fighting the Australian bully might be in her long-term interest because of the advantages that accrue to her from these 'reputation effects'; without them there might be a domino effect.

Frank's argument is that our thinking about what is in our rational interest is likely to be short-sighted; we take into account the bruises we will incur in a fight, but we are unlikely to take long-term or reputation effects into account. And this will make us prey to bullies. Furthermore, even were we to do the calculations correctly, we still would waiver in the face of short-term fears and temptations. For this reason, Frank argues, those with blind and irrational (relative to their own calculations) *commitments to revenge* will prosper in the long run and those without such commitments will lose more and more baseball bats. These irrational commitments are, for Frank, the emotions they evolved because they were selected for; Kirk is wiser than Spock after all!

But, we suggest, it's simplistic to believe that the child should *always* fight for her bat; it is sometimes irrational to fight for it even with the most long-range view. Suppose the Australian bully had an AK47 and the child failed to take that into account because of her 'irrational commitment'? One suspects her interests—long and short—would suffer. So Frank's 'commitment' to revenge can't be both an absolute commitment to *behavior* and rational at once. We shall return to this objection, but first we shall develop Frank's model further.

Frank's story has yet more complications. In order to profit from her willingness to fight, our little girl would have to let potential bullies know her commitment to the bat before there was a fight—this is the only way that her courage would pay off. Hence, for Frank *expressions* of emotions are necessary and will be selected for as aspects of the commitments that emotions are. Of course, where there is a sincere expression there can be a counterfeit, and the balance between counterfeits and sincere expressions that will lead to a stable system is part of his account. So Frank's theory is made up of a complex dance of irrational urges and expressions, both deceptive and genuine.

There is much for us to agree with Frank about. We and he see irrational behavior as the hallmark of the emotions. But we think that Frank's account is too complex, and his notion of the sorts of things that carry commitment is unnecessarily narrow. We believe that a much simpler account can preserve Frank's valuable insights that apparently irrational behaviors can be adaptive and that emotions are irrational. And we think this can be done without exposing the poor girl to the AK47s.

We shall start with a simpler account of how anger might evolve;[11] anger is a central example for Frank as well as for us. We begin by noting that there is considerable evidence that "tit-for-tat" players might prosper in a competitive environment. That is, a strategy of cooperating with people until they exploit you and then retaliating in kind seems to be an Evolutionary Stable Strategy (see Axelrod, 1984). It's reasonable to assume, then, that any proximate mechanism that would induce a person to behave in a *roughly* tit-for-tat manner will survive and prosper. In particular, we assume that a motivational system (or set of systems) that led people to *want to be* helpful to strangers in trouble, nice to people who are likely (from reputation or appearance or best of all past behavior) to be nice, and nasty to people who are known to have been nasty (or appear likely to be nasty) will result in tit-for-tat, and hence would evolve. Perhaps, then, what evolved was simply a desire for revenge against wrong doers (as well as an inclination to be nice to strangers). This is a rather simple account of the evolutionary basis of anger—it does not postulate irrational acts, expressions, mimicry, and so on. Frank considered this simpler evolutionary account and rejected it (Frank, 1988, pp. 29–37). Why?

He believes that selection for tit-for-tat could produce only *sham* altruists, and Frank is interested in accounting for the development of genuine altruism. Why does he believe this?

Frank invites us to consider the perfectly rational player who decided to play tit-for-tat and who is playing against another perfectly rational player also playing tit-for-tat. If such a player knows, for example, that this trial is the last, then rationally that player will defect on this trial, since the player need not fear retaliation; there is no tomorrow. Now consider the next-to-last trial. The perfectly rational player knows that her perfectly rational opponent will defect on the next (last) trial, so she might as well defect on this, next-to-last trial. And so it goes. Notoriously, then, tit-for-tat will not work as a strategy to induce cooperation if there are a finite number of trials known to all parties in advance. More generally, a consideration of this case shows us that if tit-for-tat evolved as a *strategy* adopted by rational actors for prudential reasons, then (a) it isn't an account of genuine altruism (or vengefulness, for that matter); and (b) it can't explain why the little girl would fight the bully leaving for Australia in the afternoon. This is why Frank rejects the evolution of tit-for-tat as an account of the evolution of altruism. And since (a) we, like Frank, believe in genuine altruism (and we certainly believe in genuine vengefulness); and (b) we believe that *some* little girls would fight the bully, and that lots more little girls would want to, tit-for-tat as a prudent strategy does seem inadequate as the account of the evolution of emotions.

We have, however, a simpler solution than Frank's. Evolution works through proximate mechanisms. If tit-for-tat is a stable and advantageous strategy, then any mechanism that results in people's playing tit-for-tat will be selected for, and, indeed, since evolution is rough and ready, any mechanism that leads people to play something like tit-for-tat will be selected for. So, suppose the following mechanism evolved: a system that leads us to want to be nice to people who are nice and to want to be mean to people who are mean (with a bias toward being nice to strangers). How will such a system do? Will it lead to tit-for-tat (or something like it)?

Well, it will give us the appropriate urges to play tit-for-tat. If we go with these urges we will cooperate with cooperators and defect against defectors—not because we have calculated that doing such is in our long-term interest but because we are going with our feelings. So an account that suggests that urges evolved does not explain away altruism as only apparent—desires aren't strategies; feelings are sincere. Note that we will also *want to* retaliate even when the person is leaving for Australia in the morning or, for that matter, has an AK47.

Nonetheless, despite these urges, we may not retaliate because other considerations may be more important than our immediate feelings. But as many people who speculate about humans and evolution have pointed out, it is probably better to think about evolution as directly implicated in *desire* rather than behavior. Thus, on our account, desire can be as irrational as you like; you can indeed want to take revenge on the Australian bully *even if he has an AK47*. But wanting revenge isn't the same as taking revenge. In the case of the AK47, it isn't dangerous to want revenge, so long as that desire doesn't inevitably lead to actually taking revenge. The desire to beat up the bully is just one desire in the pot of desires. Of course, Frank might argue that wanting unconnected from behavior has no use and won't evolve. But, we reply, wanting (contingently) leads to doing. *And that's all that is necessary.*

So we propose (following Aristotle, 1941) that humans evolved with a motivation system that causes us to experience an impulse toward revenge caused by the perception of transgression. (This is half of the system we need to be true altruists.) This *desire for* revenge is insensitive to contextual details such as: Is the bully leaving for Australia? Does he have a gun? Do I really care about this silly bat? Though the *taking of revenge* might well be somewhat sensitive to those matters, aren't we just offering a variant of Frank's account of the evolution of the emotions?

We would argue not. The desire for revenge for having perceived a transgression is, we suggest, in some circumstances (correctly) called moral indignation, outrage, an impulse toward justice, even envy (see Sabini & Silver, 1982). What distinguishes these various psychological states is not whether the perception of transgression—desire for revenge system is activated, but, rather, circumstances. If she really was traduced, then moral indignation might be in order; if she is making a mountain out of a molehill, then we would call what she was doing emotional. Also, we have a different answer than Frank does to this question: Why does the little girl want to beat up the returning-to-Australia bully?

Frank wants to argue that because of the myopia of rationality, we evolved 'commitments' as a kind of corrective lens. It is good for us (in the evolutionary long run) to be Kirk rather than Spock.

It is good for us, essentially, because of reputation effects. So in seeing the little girl's desire to beat up the visiting bully we are seeing how exquisitely evolution has shaped our mental lives. But we would propose quite the reverse. We would suggest that the reason that evolution led to a little girl inclined to (or, perhaps, half inclined to) fight for her bat is that evolved motivational systems are sloppy. They aren't precisely tuned; they are crudely tuned. They cause us to want things that are usually, but certainly not always, in our (long-term) interest.

We suggest that this crudeness is a part of all of our motivational systems. Take hunger, for instance. Believing ourselves to be on diets and that our long-term best interest is served by eating less does not make us less hungry. Knowing that—for any one of a variety of reasons—it is not in our long-term interest to have sex with a particular other makes that other no less alluring. Even curiosity can lead us to places we know we shouldn't go. Would it were so that by knowing that something was bad for us we could turn off our desires to have it. But then we would be Vulcans and have no emotions. *It is our argument that it is the fact that none of our desires are shut down by the knowledge that we shouldn't satisfy them that is the behavioral and experiential basis for our being creatures with emotions.* We do, of course, have *some* ability to refrain from acting on those motives on some occasions, but even then, as we have said, the motives make their presence felt. Perhaps evolution hasn't fixed those problems with our motivational systems (yet) because it "costs too much" to fix them. Maybe it is hard to evolve from a human to a Vulcan! Let us return to the girl, the bat, and the bully.

For us, the fact that she becomes enraged when the bully takes her bat happens because she inherited an anger system. The anger system, following Aristotle (1941), causes her to want revenge when she has been transgressed against. She got this system because creatures with it tend to play something like tit-for-tat. But, we suggest, the degree to which she wants revenge is not in the slightest modulated to how good for her it would be to try to get it. (Rather, the intensity of her desire is related to how transgressed against she has been.) Of course, as she ages she will develop (one hopes) an increasing ability to decide whether she wants to fight the bully, and an increasing ability to bring her behavior under the control of her decisions. But this is not to say that she will ever stop wanting revenge. And, contra Frank, we would not tell her that when she feels angry at people, but thinks it unwise to express that anger, she is probably *wrong,* that she probably should lash out; we would not tell her that her anger is her genes' way of lighting her path to long-term rationality.

We have been telling an "overwhelmed with desire" or at least a "paying a price for desire" story of emotion, yet a central case of being overwhelmed seems not to be about emotion at all. If our assistant professor is sitting at the meeting struggling, not with the urge to attack a senior colleague, but with the urge to attack the box of pastries, he would not be described as being in an emotional state. But perhaps this is because the language marks a distinction between desires for fairly concrete things—chocolate eclairs—and for less concrete things—prestige, justice, and so on. Perhaps getting carried away in the concrete cases isn't called emotion while in the latter cases it is.[12] In any event, this is *not* a way our story differs from Frank's. Frank seems comfortable with this distinction too, since it would appear that for him all desires except those for creature comforts are emotional, in need of explanations via the path of limited rationality and then commitments.[13]

Buck's Prime Theory

Ross Buck (1985) proposed an integrated theory of motivation and emotion that, like our theory, took the view that there was only one substantive kind of thing there. Buck, however, did not identify that kind of thing with either motivation or emotion, but rather called it a 'prime.' Primes are homeostatic mechanisms. Since Buck, like us, argues that there really is only one thing, he must, also like us, explain why people, and psychological theorists, speak sometimes of motivation and sometimes of emotion. He must, like us, say what the real phenomena that give rise to emotion talk are, and why they are spoken of as emotion.

Buck distinguishes the "action-in-the-world" functions of the primes from the "read-out" functions of the primes. He designates the former as motivational phenomena and the latter as emotional phenomena. So all those things that happen inside a person fleeing a bear, which are designed (by natural selection) to get the chap out of harm's way, are motivational phenomena, but the mechanisms that allow the person (or someone else) to know that he is in that motivational state are emotional phenomena. We have a different view.

Our position is that the reason we have evolved a discourse of emotion in addition to one of motivation is to pick out cases in which motivation fights reason. We do not share Buck's position on an evolved system to "read out" motivational (or emotional states). A person, we suggest, who has been insulted and finds himself plotting revenge has no need for a specialized system to inform him that he is angry. It is plain as day to him, just as it would be to anyone else who had access to his churning gut and stream of caustic remarks flowing past consciousness.[14] And it isn't so clear that a "read out" to others of our motivational states is such a hot idea, either; it is at least plausible to imagine that our expressive equipment evolved to misinform others of our intentions as well as to inform them. This is not to say, however, that facial expressions didn't evolve for reasons of social interaction. We will have more to say about this in the section on Darwin below. In summary, then, like Buck, we agree that there really is only one kind of thing in the motivational/emotional domain. For Buck, however, the two aspects of that kind of thing—emotion and motivation—had separate evolutionary paths. We suggest a simpler idea. The one kind of thing is motivation.

Lazarus, Motivation and Emotion

Richard Lazarus (1991) also attempts to disentangle emotions and motives. Like Peters (1972), he sees appraisals as central to both; like Buck, he sees emotions and motives as parts of a complex. Lazarus, however, stands Buck on his head. For Buck, emotions are aspects of motives, read-outs; for Lazarus, motives are necessary components of emotions.

On Lazarus's account, in order to have an emotion we must appraise our environment in light of the ways in which the situation allows us to realize (or prevents us from realizing) our goals. We then attempt to, or at least experience an urge to, achieve the particular benefit (or avoid the particular harm). This attempt, which involves 'activation' and 'goal direction', is what Lazarus means by 'motivation'. Each emotion involves this activation and goal direction resulting from an appraisal, but the emotion is more complex: "In sum, motivation in nature is a fusion of activation and goal direction, just as emotion is a fusion of motivation, knowledge, and appraisal of the person environment relationship." Lazarus also states, "Emotions occur only when a motivational stake has been appraised" (p. 172). What Lazarus is claiming is that emotions involve bringing together general knowledge of the world and more specific knowledge of how a situation affects us, along with coping strategies, our appraisal of the stakes involved, and how our esteem and prospects are affected and, in addition to that, perhaps, a second-order reaction to the likelihood of our success or failure.

As interesting as this position is, it has some counterintuitive results. Consider, if you will, our assistant professor hearing for the fiftieth time about what life was like when giants roamed the earth. Suppose he lashed out, "You fatuous fool, can't we have one meeting where we don't hear about what life was like at the dawn of creation?" Is this person in an emotional state? Not according to Lazarus.

According to Lazarus, the assistant professor, here, isn't in an emotional state because he hasn't appraised the broad relationship he has to his environment—though he is in a motivational state. In order to get from motivation to emotion he needs to distance himself from his immediate desires and impulses, at least enough to assess his position broadly. It is an odd result that if you haven't stepped back from what you immediately want to do you *can't* be emotional as a conceptual matter.

But it is not by accident that Lazarus finds himself with this counterintuitive result. He, like us, needs to distinguish emotion from motivation. He finds this distinction in a kind of second-order appraisal (if we understand his distinction between the appraisal inherent in motivation and the knowledge and appraisal that must be added to it to get an emotion). His theory, however, is better suited to the self-regarding emotions like shame or pride than to the passions. We, of course, have no objection to the view that emotions, like pride and shame, do indeed involve the kind of appraisal Lazarus speaks of. We are not convinced, however, either that anger involves such a second-order appraisal or that anger isn't an emotion. Given that, we need to find a distinction between the motivation of anger and the emotion of anger elsewhere.

THE BOOSTER ROCKET THEORY

There is one view of the relation of emotion to motivation that seems present in Lazarus's theory, and in Frank's,[15] but seems to be an aspect of other theorists' positions as well—a view we think might be called the booster-rocket theory of emotions. This is a theory that attempts to account for the emotions as elements of our mental economy that evolved because they *intensify* motivation.

Booster-rocket theories assert that in the beginning there were motivations. Desires, say, for revenge or self-esteem evolved because they are good for us. But, the booster-rocket theory says, these motivations were too weak (for some reason) to do us the best good they could. So then, on top of these motives, something else evolved—emotions—to boost our motivational levels to a better, higher level. The emotions are the final stage of the motivational rocket, the one that gets us into orbit.

A related view of the emotions and their functions is that the emotions aren't so much rockets as they are sirens we can't turn off. The idea here, again, is that we have motives, but natural selection wasn't wise enough to make our motives strong or pressing enough, so we profited from a device that rivets our attention to our activated motives. Emotions are this device.

The analogy here is to pain. If you step on a thorn, you might not be inclined to remove it in time to prevent tissue damage. But pain evolved so as to rivet your attention to the thorn problem and to send you in search of Saint Jerome now (before you have an infection) rather than later (when it is too late). Well, the argument goes, so it is with emotion.

We have two comments on such theories. First, they seem unnecessarily complex. Why posit whimpy motives and then emotions to fix that problem? Is there any independent reason to imagine that our desires are too weak? But this is a minor complaint. The serious issue is that any such theory needs to be thoroughly explicit about the difference between motivation and emotion so we can tell whether the booster rocket has kicked in (or we are just seeing the second stage's effects) or the siren is on (or we are just hearing the motivation).

We suspect there is no way to be explicit about this because the only difference to be found between emotion and motivation is one of degree. We suspect that the stronger the motive, the more likely one is to perceive the presence of emotion. This *isn't,* we propose, because there is something in the mental economy—emotion—that kicks in to boost motivation, but because as a *linguistic matter* it is only *excessive* motivation that is called emotion. In any event, it would seem that those who subscribe to either the booster-rocket or warning-siren views of emotion need to find a way to distinguish emotion from motivation, under pain of being question begging.

Action and Emotion

Recently Nico Frijda and Ira Roseman (Frijda, Kuipers, & ter Shure, 1989; Roseman, Wiest, & Swartz, 1994) have made arguments very close to our own. Frijda has shown that subjects identify particular emotions with both particular appraisals and specific action readinesses. And Roseman has also shown that the emotions are associated with distinctive action tendencies even in the absence of overt action. So for both of these theorists, fear, for example, is a tendency to withdraw caused by an appraisal of danger. Indeed, Roseman (Roseman, Wiest, & Swartz, 1994) writes of "emotional motives" which he terms 'emotivations'. Emotivational states are, it seems, just like the "traditional" motives of hunger, thirst, and need for achievement. Indeed, the only thing unclear in this analysis is just how the emotivational states are to be distinguished from the motivational ones!

We would suggest there is no useful way to distinguish them. We would suggest that motivational states and emotional states are the same states—at least for the limited set of emotions connected to the passions.

Consensus View

Recently, Paul Ekman and Richard Davidson have gathered a group of scholars to write about the nature of emotion (Ekman & Davidson, 1994). Different scholars have, of course, different views of the emotions, but Ekman and Davidson note that there is consensus on some matters. One matter of consensus is, they write, that emotions are motivational in that they "organize behavioral and physiological patterns to deal with emotion evoking events. . . . Emotions have motivational properties in that people attempt to maximize positive emotions and minimize negative emotions" (p. 412).

These are, of course, two quite different ideas about emotion and motivation. Organizing physiological and behavioral responses to deal with the world is the role usually assigned to motivation; this is, for example, what one imagines the hunger drive does: it organizes behavioral and physiological responses to deal with the internal and external environment. Since we argue that emotions are, at heart, motives, we are hardly likely to disagree with Ekman and Davidson about this; we just wonder whether, and if so why, they think that emotions are entities distinct from motives but that nonetheless have "motivational properties".

In the second sense, emotions are tied to motivation because emotional states are reinforcers. It is argued that we do things in order to get into or out of emotional states. Perhaps we do sometimes, even for the passions. But, we would suggest, the main connection between anger and motivation is *not* that we sometimes do things in order to become (or be less) angry, but that when we are angry at fatuous colleagues we want to punch them in the nose. Our state of anger is a motivational state. (And, specifically, we find it hard to believe that jealousy evolved because of its role as a negative reinforcer!)

In our view, emotions per se have no functions. They are not the sorts of thing that could have a function. This is our primary difference with the authors and editors of the Ekman and Davidson volume (1994). The functions proposed in that volume include recruiting physiological changes to support adaptive behavior, preparing us to engage in specific actions that have survival value, changing our motives (specifically the goals we seek), focusing and, therefore, perhaps interfering with cognition. A number, but not all, of the contributors, did comment on when emotions were dysfunctional—for example, when they are expressed out of context, or prolonged beyond a useful duration, but nonetheless, there was a consensus, one from which we demur, that emotions per se are functional.

Emotions and Passions

We have limited our discussion so far to emotions that are connected to the passions; a test for whether something belongs in that category is whether a person can be said both to be x (or feel x) and act out of x (where by 'act' one means engage in goal direction action—i.e., act on a motive). So one may both be afraid (or free afraid) and act out of fear. And so too it is for envy, jealousy, and anger—at least. But it is *not* so for, say, sadness (or joy, awe, regret, or embarrassment).[16] One may, to be sure, fail to act because one is sad—but that isn't the same thing as acting out of sadness. For example, one might be so overwhelmed with sadness that one fails to show up for work. But to say this is to say that the person's absence from work was the failure to achieve a goal, not the accomplishment of a goal. And one may surely avoid doing something in order to avoid the experience of sadness, and in *that* sense sadness may be motivating, but that's not to say sadness is a desire. (There is a difference between going to the supermarket on the weekend to avoid hunger on Tuesday evening and wolfing down a pan of brownies because one is ravenous. And it isn't a matter of degree.) But if sadness and anger are such different kinds of things, why are both called emotions?[17]

We think the common element is *disruption*—disruption of goal-directed activity, but also, perhaps, of reveries. Let us consider some examples. Shame and embarrassment, two prominent emotions, obviously involve disruption. One is overcome with shame or embarrassment; in some universities, there is a tradition that students applaud the professor at the end of the last class. The first time this happens to you it is embarrassing, but one gets used to it. Still, it is rude not to look embarrassed. What, we suggest, distinguishes the real embarrassment the first time from the mock embarrassment the twentieth is the fact that one really is taken aback—disrupted—for the first time, but not the twentieth. Some of the other emotions clearly involve disruption. But what about, say, joy?

Well, one does jump for joy and jumping is a disruption of most goal-directed actions. But most joy doesn't lead to jumping—only the most intense does. And most sadness doesn't lead to weeping and gnashing of teeth. What about the milder states of joy or sadness that make them, nonetheless, emotions? Well, for one thing, joy and sadness do intrude into one's thinking, and in that sense they are disruptive. But other things intrude on our consciousness, too—grocery lists, for example—and they aren't emotional. How are joy and sadness different from grocery lists?

For one thing, joy and sadness have hedonic consequences for the rest of life. A sad person is able to take less pleasure than he used to in a variety of things; a joyous person can take more. From the point of view of a person as a bundle of projects, plans, and activities, joy and sadness with their attendant changes in hedonics and the distractions the hedonics bring with them are disruptions—welcome disruptions, perhaps, but disruptions nonetheless.

What Spock Lacks: The Place of the Emotions

There is a strong intuition that Spock lacks something—something important to being human. There is a strong intuition that it is a good thing that we have emotions. But there is certainly nothing about *our* analysis of the emotions that would recommend them. Can we reconcile the intuition with our analysis?

As it happens in humans, we suggest, strong and sincere desire often (though not always) gives rise to the symptoms of emotion—obsession, inappropriate action, distraction, and so on. Therefore we use these signs in deciding (about others and even ourselves) what people really care about (see chapter 3). But this is an empirical fact about us humans; it is not a conceptual fact. One can imagine a species in which parents, say, care about their offspring in the sense that they are willing to sacrifice everything, including their lives, but they do not experience the other signs of emotion. In such a species we would surely agree that the parents authentically care about their offspring, even in the absence of emotion. Thus, there is no conceptual tie between caring about something and experiencing emotions with regard to it, though there just as surely is an empirical tie in the case of us poor humans. It is our claim, then, that the emotions are important because they have empirical connection to authentic desire. Those authentic desires are important per se, the emotions aren't.

Notes

1. This chapter will for the most part be agnostic about the existence of the other emotions, but its authors are more skeptical than agnostic.

2. Commonsense philosophers and cognitive scientists affected by common sense tend to use 'desire'. Psychologists have tended to use 'motivation'. We shall use those words interchangeably as theoretical

and abstract terms. Hunger (a motivation) consists, among other things, of a desire to eat.

3. Of course, it might be true as a matter of fact that unless one has certain emotions, one can't be, say, loyal. We know of no evidence on this score, however. At the very least, there seems to be no conceptual problem with an emotionless but loyal person.

4. There is a famous debate in the history of psychology about whether the emotions organize or disorganize action. In our account they do neither. Disorganized actions are likely to be talked of as emotional; organized actions are less likely to be seen as emotional. Of course, that is not to say that *motivation* or *desire* doesn't organize or disorganize action. But that is an old, old story told in the Yerkes-Dodson law.

5. Suppose instead he said, "Yes, I agree it will make it less likely that I will get tenure. But it is not worth it to be an academic if I have to grovel. And, as you may recall from the letters people wrote about me when I was applying for a job here, I have never borne fools lightly." Now, we suggest, insofar as anyone is persuaded that he indeed decided to lash out will again withdraw that characterization. He has made what he did rational by showing that a broader assessment of all he wants from life makes this the right (or, perhaps a right) act. Now another case. All is the same as above, except that the observer knows that this person has not had a history of fighting for independence. And, in fact, he is typically quite accommodating. Now, though the observer may believe that he decided to lash out, and that he sincerely believes his decision was based on his values—as it was in the previous case—such an informed observer would continue to believe that his decision itself was driven by emotion, was emotional. Such are the complexities.

6. On this account, Vulcans do not experience regret. If a crew member must be sacrificed to save the ship, both a human and a Vulcan officer would be likely to do it. We could expect the human to be tormented by his action, to think back to the horror he has caused. If he did not, we would see him as cold—in fact, not having the appropriate attachment to his crew. The Vulcan would do the rational thing, expect others to do the rational thing (if he were a crew member), and that would be it—it would make no sense to him to regret his decision. This does not mean, however, that the Vulcan does not care about his

crew member while Kirk does. Indeed, the Vulcan captain might do anything he could to save his crew member if he thought he could—and *that* surely is the acid test for caring.

7. Of course, instincts are also innate rather than acquired. But that is irrelevant to the point at hand; what is relevant is that instincts guide goal-directed behavior.

8. Actually, their theory is explicitly about what happens when a person is in a state of "unexplained arousal." That, presumably, isn't the usual case when someone experiences an emotion. Still, it is possible to recast their theorizing in more general terms and to treat it as a theory of emotion tout court. And textbook writers are inclined to do that (see Sabini, 1995, for example). Still, it is unfair to hold Schachter and Singer responsible for other people's generalizing.

9. Of course, maybe that's because their theory is really only about what they say it's about, cases in which people experience unexplained arousal because something odd happened to them—for example, they just got a shot of adrenaline masquerading as a vitamin, Suproxin.

10. Frank's account is meant to apply to a broader class of emotions than just anger. Our theory is meant to apply only to the passions. Anger is a central case for us and it is for him, so it is the natural meeting point for this discussion.

11. Frank does not sharply distinguish emotion from motivation. Perhaps this is because he sees all behavior that serves noneconomic motives as irrational and hence emotional.

12. We take this concrete-abstract distinction with regard to the objects of desire to be the same distinction as a sensory-cognitive distinction in terms of the mental faculties needed to apprehend the object. So no fancy thinking is needed to grow hungry on smelling bacon frying, but some cognition will be needed to understand as fatuous one's colleague's utterances.

13. Frank sees the desire for revenge against the marauding bully, for example, as an irrational desire. For him it is precisely because it is irrational but adaptive that it evolved as an emotion. But we would be hard pressed to defend the rationality (or irrationality) of *any* desire. Of course, one can defend the rationality of desires that are for intermediate goals—it is rational to want an umbrella if one wants to keep

dry and it is raining. But there is something strange about asking whether it is rational to want to have sex with someone. Wanting to have sex with someone isn't the sort of thing that is rational or irrational. Doing so (or not doing so) might be, but it is the doing, not the wanting, that gets judged as rational. We have the same attitude about revenge. Wanting to take revenge against someone who has crossed you is, we suggest, neither rational nor irrational; it is human, perhaps all too human.

14. This is not to say the person has *infallible* knowledge of his emotional state. On the other hand, Buck does grant the individual incorrigible knowledge of his emotional state. We suggest that knowledge of one's state is inferential—often a damned fine inference, and, hence, fallible.

15. Frank's theory isn't exactly a booster-rocket theory because, as far as we can tell, for Frank all desires for nonsurvival goods are "emotional." But if one were to adjust Frank's theory so as to claim that there evolved motivations for revenge, and the emotions evolved to solve the commitment problem, then one would have a booster-rocket theory of emotion.

16. We have said nothing about love. That is the topic of a paper of its own, but it is worth pointing out in this context that love has features of both sorts of emotion.

17. If we believe that 'emotion' is a classical concept you will want to know what features these kinds of things share. If you believe that 'emotion' has prototype structure, then this question is fuzzed up, but it doesn't go away. Prototype theorists (see Russell, 1991, for the prototype) believe that the concept emotion has no necessary and/or sufficient features. But such theorists do believe that the prototype itself has features that are important to it qua prototype. And that leads one to ask: Why *those* features and not others? After all, the feature "amusing for a cat to watch" isn't part of the prototype of 'anger', but why? Is it really all random?

Anger, for example, admits of both an episodic and a dispositional sense. So, though one may be (rightly) said to have been angry with one's brother-in-law for 20 years, one surely does not mean by that that one has experienced a 20-year episode of anger. But, to be sure, episodes slide off into dispositions without clean breaks.

References

Aristotle. (1941). *The rhetoric, Book 2. The basic works of Aristotle.* R. McKeon (Ed.) New York: Random House.

Axelrod, R. (1984). *The evolution of cooperation.* New York: Basic Books.

Buck, R. (1985). Prime theory: An integrated view of motivation and emotion. *Psychological Review, 92,* 389–413.

Dewey, J. (1895). The theory of emotion. II. The significance of emotions. *Psychological Review, 2,* 13–32.

Ekman, P. (1973). Cross-cultural studies of facial expression. In P. Ekman (Ed.), *Darwin and facial expression.* New York: Academic Press.

Ekman, P., & Davidson, R. J. (Eds.). (1994). *The nature of emotion: Fundamental questions.* New York: Oxford University Press.

Frank, R. H. (1988). *Passions within reason: The strategic role of the emotions.* New York: Norton.

Frijda, N. H., Kuipers, P., & ter Schure, E. (1989). Relations among emotions, appraisal, and emotional action readiness. *Journal of Personality and Social Psychology, 57,* 212–228.

James, W. (1890/1950). *Principles of psychology,* Vol. 2. New York: Holt.

Lazarus, R. S. (1991). *Emotion and adaptation.* New York: Oxford University Press.

Marshall, G. D., & Zimbardo, P. G. (1979). Affective consequences of inadequately explained physiological arousal. *Journal of Personality and Social Psychology, 37,* 970–988.

Maslach, C. (1979). Negative emotional biasing of unexplained arousal. *Journal of Personality and Social Psychology, 37,* 953–969.

Peters, R. S. (1972). The education of the emotions. In R. F. Deaden, P. H. Hirst, & R. S. Peters (Eds.), *Education and the development of reason* (pp. 466–483). London: Routledge & Kegan Paul.

Roseman, I. J., Wiest, C., & Swartz, T. S. (1994). Phenomenology, behaviors, and goals differentiate discrete emotions. *Journal of Personality and Social Psychology, 67,* 206–221.

Russell, J. A. (1991). In defense of a prototype approach to emotion concepts. *Journal of Personality and Social Psychology, 60,* 37–47.

Sabini, J. (1995). *Social Psychology*, 2nd ed. New York: Norton.
Sabini, J., & Silver, M. (1982). *Moralities of everyday life*. New York: Oxford University Press, 15–35.
Schachter, S., & Singer, J. (1962). Cognitive, social, and physiological determinants of emotional state. *Psychological Review, 69*, 379–399.

Index

Adams, R. M., 20
admiration, as both moral and aesthetic, 23
aesthetic judgments
　of character, 18–25, 98
　nature of, 24–25
　as opposed to pragmatic judgments, 19
　and revulsion as opposed to blame, 19
altruism, 147–151
anger
　abstract causes of and responses to, 14
　episodic and dispositional sense of, 59–60

Frank's evolution theory of emotions and, 144–151
appraisals, as necessary to emotions and motives, 14, 139–140
Arendt, Hanna., 26n1
Aristotle, 14, 17, 18, 78,
　on morality and the good life, 27n5
　and *Nichomachean Ethics*, 17, 26n3
　on psychology of the emotions, 14, 150
　on responsibility for emotions, 17–18, 101n10

Beecher, H. K., 50n6
beliefs, 99n2
Benedict, R., and shame and guilt cultures, 93–95
betrayal. *See* loyalty
Block, N., 51n9
Blum, R., 20, 27n6
Buck, R., and the theory of primes in motives and emotions, 151–153

Camus, Albert. *See Strange, The*
Canfield, J. and Gustavson, G., 106
caring
   as beyond the will, 31–49. *See also* passivity
   and emotions, 37–39
   without emotions, 38–39
   and pain, 35–37
   pain without, 36, 50n6
   relation between sympathy and, 31–51
   and values, 40–49
Champlain, T. S., 106, 109, 123
character
   aesthetics of, 19–25, 27n5, 98
      as a basis of admiration and criticism, 23–24
      and integrity, 22–23
      and moral sincerity, 23
      and shame, 98
      and supererogatory acts, 22
   and emotion, 18–25
   and guilt and shame, 88–89
   judgments of, 19–25, 27n
   moral as opposed to aesthetic aspects of, 9–30
   and pragmatic considerations, 19
   and voluntarism, 93
   and will, 9–10, 20
commitment, Franks's theory of, 145–146
consequentialism. *See* utilitarianism
continuity
   as an aesthetic virtue, 21
   as part of a complete theory of self, 20–21

Dennett, D. C., 36
desires. *See* motives
dramaturgy
   and feeling guilty, 86–87
   incomplete as model of sincerity, 53–54, 64–65
   and sincerity, 53–66
   See also Goffman, E.
duty
   disharmony between desires and, 26n1, 77–78
   and friendship, 72–78
   as too impersonal to support relationships, 70
   as opposed to compassion as a source of action, 15
   See also Kantian view of emotions

Ekman, P., and R., Davidson, 157–158

Index 169

Elster, J., 124
embarrassment
　without discrediting facts, 96
　and dramaturgic flaws, 96–97
　as requiring an audience, 96
　and shame, 95–98
emotional behavior
　as the disruption of goal-directed behavior, 159
　as sensible but unwise, 133–134, 161n5
emotional experience
　as a manifestation of aroused desire, 135
　as private, 134–136
emotion concepts
　dispositional and episodic uses of, 6, 59–60
　disruption of goal-directed behavior as criterion for, 159
　and prototypes, 163n17
emotions
　and caring, 37–39, 160
　and character, 18–25
　and choice, 9, 10, 14–18, 25, 32, 37–41, 61, 92, 93, 135, 139–140
　and commonsense psychology, 130–136
　and the disorganization of behavior, 161n4
　and distortions in judgment, 116
　as distractions from duty (Kant), 10, 26n1
　as not elements of the mental life, 129–165

　and ethics and aesthetics, 22–25
　as goal of self-deception, 110–111
　and irrationality, 38, 144–147, 162n13
　as motives, 129–134
　　acted upon despite decision not to, 133–134, 136, 161n5
　　experienced but not acted upon, 133–134, 136, 161n5
　the pain model of, 9–13
　as passive, 5, 14–17, 139–140
　as requiring appraisals, 14, 139–140, 99n2
　role of in Turing test, 3–4
　and sincerity, 58–61
　and sympathy for someone, 37–40
　and the will, 39–40, 135
emotions, theories of
　booster rocket theory, 154–156
　Buck, R., and prime theory, 151–153
　Dewey, J., and conflict theory, 136–139
　Ekman, P., and R. Davidson and "the consensus view," 157–158
　and fallacy of misplaced concreteness, 13–14
　Frank, R., and an evolutionary theory, 144–151

Frijda, N., and I. Roseman and two accounts of emotions as action readiness, 156
James, W.
  theory of emotions as instincts, 137–138
  theory of emotions as perceptions of a bodily state, 11, 137–138
Lazarus, R., and motivational states, 153–154
Peters, R. S., and emotions as appraisals leading to passive phenomena, 139–140
psychophysical model, 12
and qualia, 12–14
Schacter, S., and J. Singer and emotions and unexplained arousal, 12, 140–144
Tomkins, S., and facial feedback and emotions, 12
Zajonc, R., and emotions as noncognitive, 11, 12
entrapment and slippery slopes, 118
envy
  abstract sources of and responses to, 14
  and culpability, 109
evolution of motives and emotions, 144–151

faith, as opposed to self-deception, 111–112
feelings
  avowal of, and insincerity, 54–61
  as beliefs, 61–64
  and clinical judgment, 63
  connected to action in sincerity, 58
  and creating the self, 59–63
  episodic as opposed to nonepisodic senses of, 59
  and intuition, 61–64
  as outside the will, 54–61
  as tacit knowledge, 61–63
Fingarette, H., 115, 125n5
Frank, R. H., 144–151
Freud, Sigmund, 58, 112, 124n1
friendship
  and duty, 75–78
  and embodiment of the good, 72
  and Kantian theory, 69–70, 75–78
  and shared history, 73–75
  and ulterior motives, 71–73
  See also love
Frijda, N., 156

Gardner, P., 111–112
Goffman, Erving., 53–54, 87, 121n1, 126
good life, the, 69
guilt
  when not commensurate with shame, 88–89
  connection of with shame, 88
  as constructive emotion (Tangney), 89–92
  possibility of, without shame, 89–93
  and shame cultures, 93–95

and ways different from
shame, 87–88
weakness of, 92–93
See also shame
guilt, feeling of
without fault, 86–87, 100n4, 100n5
and feeling ashamed, 83–84, 85–86, 99n3
and moral responsibility, 85–86
as opposed to being guilty, 82–83
as not unique feeling, 83, 99n1

Hamlyn, D., 122, 123
Hinman, L., 20 on emotions necessary to doing one's duty, 27n4
human, the
purposes of as opposed to computer purposes, 41–45
Turing test for, and the emotions, 3–4
human nature choice as opposed to emotion as central to, 4–5
humiliation, 21
hypocrisy, 123

impartiality
and aesthetic judgments of character, 19–20
and friendship, 75–78

as precluding love and loyalty, 5–6, 69–70, 75–78
impulses
and the discovery of the self, 67n4
and sincerity, 56–58
unexpressed, and the construction of self, 58
and values, 57–58
insincerity. *See* sincerity
integrity as involving both moral and aesthetic judgments, 22–23
intuition, 61–64
and algorithms, 63, 67n6

James, William, 11, 137–139
Joyce, James. *See Ulysses*.

Kant, Immanuel, 5, 10–11, 13, 23, 69, 122,
and continuity of the self, 20–21
on loyalty, 75–78
Kantian view of emotions, the
and the absence of moral significance of the emotions, 9–11, 26n1, 69–70
limitations of, 15–16
and 'moral schizophrenia', 70, 75–78
Kekes, H. N., 20

Lazarus, R., 153–154
Lineham, E., 109, 123

linguistic (conceptual) approach,
    to sincerity, 66n
    to sympathy, 32
love, 69–78
    and commitment, 70–71
    as embodiment of good, 72
    and shared history, 73–74
    of someone in particular, 72–73
    and ulterior motives, 71–7
    and utilitarianism, 69–75
loyalty
    despite repulsion, 77–78
    as a duty to a particular person, 75–77
    and feelings, 131, 161n3
    as generalizable, 76
    and impartiality, 5–6, 69–70, 70–78
    and Kant, 75–78
    and shared history, 73–75
    and shared projects, 74–75
    and utilitarianism, 73–75

Marañon, G., 11
Melzack, R., 50n6
Miceli, M., 124
Miedaner, T., 49n2
Milgram, S., 66
Moore, G. E., 71–72
moral judgments
    and blame as opposed to revulsion, 19, 20
    and character judgments, 19–20
    and emotions, 15–18

moral reproach, for aesthetic as well as moral failings, 22
'moral schizophrenia'(Stocker), 16, 69–70, 74
motivational systems, sloppiness of, and emotional experience, 150
motives
    and appraisals, 139–140
    as entities, 129–135
    and emotions (passions) picked out by same word, 132–133

objectivity
    and judgments of character, 9
    and morality, 69

pain
    as beyond the will, 36–37, 50n7
    and caring, 35–37, 50–51n8
    as a model of the emotions, 9–13, 155–156
    and sincerity, 55–56
    and sympathy, 35–36
passions, the, 129–165
passivity
    and caring, 31–52
    and character, 5, 15–16, 18–22
    and human nature, 5, 31–32
    and Peters's theory of emotions, 139–140
Peters, R. S., 17, 132–133, 139–140

pragmatic judgments
　as a basis for character judgments, 19
　as contingently desirable, 19
　contrasted with moral and aesthetic judgments, 19
Presentation of Self in Everyday Life (Goffman), 124n1
purpose
　of a computer, 41–45
　full-blooded, 41–42
　levels of, 41–45

rationality
　and emotions, 38, 162n13
　and impartiality, 5
regret, 161n6
responsibility
　for emotions (Aristotle), 17–18
　and feeling guilty, 85–87
　Kantian view of in relation to emotions, 9–11
　and morality, 15–16
　as opposed to emotions in the judgment of character, 9–30
Rey, G., 37
romanticism, as stressing intuition in the creation of selves, 63–64, 66n2
Roseman, I., 156
Rousseau, Jean–Jacques, 23
　and the *Confessions*, 65–66
Ryle, G., 71

Sartre, Jean-Paul., 4–5, 17, 106, 114
Schacter, S., and J. Singer 12
　and experiment on emotion and attribution of unexplained arousal, 142–144
　theory of emotion of, 140–144
self-deception
　as aesthetic defect (flaw of character), 122–123
　contrasted with wishful thinking, 126n8
　and cooked evidence, 113–118, 25n6
　and deception about deceiving oneself, 112–118
　Freudian view of, 124n1
　Goffman's view of, 124n1
　and hypocrisy, 123
　and loyalty, 111–112
　'machine election' model of, 117, 125–126n7
　manipulation of psychological states as goal of, 110–112, 116–117, 125n6
　and moods, 119–120
　as opposed to error or deceit, 106–107
　as opposed to faith, 111–112
　role of unmotivated biases in, 118–119
　Sartre and the paradox of, 106
　as not self-contradictory, 108–109
　and slippery slopes, 118, 126n8

self-deception (*continued*)
   and unconscious processes, 120–122
   and underdiscounting, 115, 117–120
shame, 21
   when not commensurate with guilt, 88–89
   and beliefs about a discrediting situation, 99n2, 100n4
   as dependent on internalized standards, 95, 101n11
   and discrediting facts, 96
   and embarrassment, 95–98
   experience of, 84–85
   and guilt, 81, 83–86, 87, 88–98
   and guilt cultures, 93–95
   as irrational and destructive (Tangney), 89–93
   as not requiring an audience, 95
   See also guilt, embarrassment
shared history, and love, friendship, and loyalty, 73–75
sincerity
   and the antihero, 65–66
   and commitments, 57–61
   and emotions, 58–61
   and feelings, 54–61
   and impulses, 56–58
   and model of fitting avowal to experience, 54–61
   as a moral and aesthetic value, 23, 65
   and pain avowal, 55–56
   as not the same as a transparent consciousness, 55

Skinner, B. F., 44
Solomon, R., 17
Stocker, M., 20, 23, 69–79
   and critique of Kantian morality, 16, 69–70, 75–78
   and critique of utilitarianism, 71–75
   on emotions and duty, 27n4
   and love 69–79
   on 'moral schizophrenia', 16, 69–70, 74
Stranger, The (Camus), 65–66
sympathy
   and caring about
      emotions, 37–40
      pain, 35–37
      values, 40–49
   contrasted with other grounds of morality, 32–33
   as grounded in the passivity of caring, 31–49
   as moral, 49n1
Szavabados, B., 126n8

Tangney, J. P., 81, 84, 85, 89–93, 99n1
Taylor, C., 41–45
tit-for-tat strategy and the evolution of the emotions, 146–157
Tomkins, S., 12
Trilling, L. 54
Turing test
   Block critique of, 51n9
   and distinguishing between human and machine, 3–4
   role of emotions in, 3–4

Ulysses (Joyce), 54, 65
utilitarianism
  and detachable qualities, 71–75, 76
  and the good as an ulterior motive, 72–75
  Moore's, 71–72
  Stocker critique of and 'moral schizophrenia', 69–75

values
  as a form of caring, 40, 45–48, 51n10
  and impulses in sincerity, 57–58
  interfering with and suffering, 46
  terminal (ultimate), 46, 48
  tradeoff between moral and aesthetic, 21–25
Vulcans (*Star Trek*), 130–136, 150, 160, 161n6

will
  beyond the
    and caring, 31–52
    and feelings and sincerity 15–16, 54–61
  weakness of, 124n2
Williams, B., 20
Weber, M., 64

Zajonc, R., 11, 12, 121